50
HABITS OF
HIGHLY SUCCESSFUL
BUSINESS
LEADERS

THE ROADMAP TO SUCCESS
AND FULFILMENT

MATTHEW LIN

CONTENTS

ACKNOWLEDGMENTS

Crafting "50 Habits of Highly Successful Business Leaders" has truly been a team journey. I am deeply indebted to the many who support, guide and inspire me. As I share this book, I want to extend my heartfelt gratitude to those who have contributed to the realization of this project.

To the leaders whose words fill these pages, your wisdom serves as the guiding light, making the maze of leadership feel more navigable and inspiring us to aim higher.

To my mentors and advisors, your insights have kept me anchored, ensuring they remain true to the essence of leadership excellence.

To the dedicated team who worked behind the curtain—researching, writing, editing, and designing—your unwavering commitment has brought this book to life and has transformed an idea into a tangible reality that we are proud to share.

To my family, your endless support has been the backbone of this project. Your patience and faith propelled me forward during the most challenging phases.

To my readers, presenting "50 Habits of Highly Successful Business Leaders" to you is an honor. Your commitment to personal growth is a testament to the spirit of leadership. I hope these pages serve as a valuable tool in your upward journey.

Lastly, I am grateful to the universe for the serendipitous moments, experiences, and teachings that deepened our understanding of leadership. I wish this book stands as a symbol of what's possible when passion meets collaboration.

With heartfelt appreciation,
Matthew Lin

INTRODUCTION

In today's ever-evolving business landscape, bursting with opportunities yet rife with challenges, the quest for true success has never been more intense. Both budding leaders and experienced magnates are constantly seeking the formula behind the most influential figures in business. However, beyond innate talent and occasional luck, it's the daily habits of these leaders that dictate their continued success.

"50 Habits of Highly Successful Business Leaders" shines a spotlight on these essential habits gleaned from the experiences and wisdom of esteemed business personalities. Each chapter offers a glimpse into the practices and beliefs of those who have mastered leadership, arming you with tools to shape your own path to greatness.

Though our world continues to change, the essence of leadership—inspiring, innovating, and making an impact—remains the same. This book isn't just a source of inspiration; it's a manual for creating meaningful change in your professional journey.

The insights here are tailored to uplift and empower no matter where you stand in your career—be it at the helm of a multinational corporation, navigating corporate intricacies, or at the outset of a startup venture. As you delve into the stories and wisdom of those who have transformed the business world, you'll recognize that true greatness is an ongoing journey, not a final destination.

The habits detailed in this book are more than just ideas; they are practical, transformative tools ready to be woven into your daily life. Each is a building block toward achieving unparalleled professional heights. From improving communication to refining decision-making, these habits serve as both your guide and mentor.

As you navigate the world of leadership success, always remember: the habits you foster now will define the legacy you leave. With the insights of pioneers lighting your path, you're equipped to ascend to new heights, shaping not only your future but the future of the business world.

With "50 Habits of Highly Successful Business Leaders" in hand, you have the blueprint to soar and redefine success.

CHAPTER 1

Self-Mastery

Laying the Groundwork for Exceptional Leadership

I n the shifting landscape of the business world, where challenges evolve into opportunities and innovation thrives amid uncertainty, a foundational truth stands firm: To lead others, you must first lead yourself. This chapter, "Self-Mastery," paves the way for our deeper exploration into the 50 transformative habits of standout leaders.

The journey to impactful leadership isn't just about having the right qualifications or occupying an influential position. It's a voyage into the self—understanding one's essence, committing to growth, and believing unrelentingly in one's potential for enhancement. The practices discussed here aren't just theoretical; they're real, battle-tested methods that have anchored the journeys of the most triumphant leaders.

Central to self-mastery is a simple yet profound realization: our perceptions and reactions are deeply tied to our internal narratives. By embracing a growth mindset as our first habit, we acknowledge that success isn't a fixed outcome but emerges from resilience, adaptability, and an unceasing hunger for knowledge. In the words of Tony Robbins, "The only thing that's keeping you from getting what you want is the story you keep telling yourself." Through this prism, we grasp our immense potential to shape our destiny.

We then dive into personal development, unearthing Habit 2: Prioritize Personal Development. Just as the base of a building dictates its pinnacle, our depth of self-awareness defines our leadership reach. We draw upon Helmut Schmidt's insight that "The biggest room in the world is the room for improvement." With an unwavering commitment to progress, we continuously widen our horizons.

This chapter teaches us to embrace daily reflection, a ritual heralded by thinkers like Socrates. And as we traverse the tumultuous terrain of leadership, resilience, our fourth habit, becomes our unwavering compass. Echoing Winston Churchill, "success is not final, failure is not fatal; it is the courage to continue that counts." Recognizing setbacks as milestones toward our goals, we foster an indomitable spirit.

Habit 5 is the essence of time management, rounding off our self-mastery dive. Heeding Benjamin Franklin's wisdom that "You may delay, but time will not," we pledge to make every second meaningful. We focus on initiatives that mirror our greater vision by reigning in our hours.

This chapter is your invitation to self-discovery, growth, and reshaping. The habits presented aren't lofty dreams but tangible steps, ensuring your leadership stands on a bedrock of self-awareness, growth, resilience, and effective time utilization. The voyage is just setting sail; as we traverse the self-mastery terrain, we're on course to emerge as leaders who not just address today's challenges but architect tomorrow's potential.

H A B I T

CULTIVATE A GROWTH MINDSET

"The only thing that's keeping you from getting what you want is the story you keep telling yourself."

—Tony Robbins

E very individual, at its core, is both the author and the protagonist of a unique story—one that shapes their world, their aspirations, and their destiny. At the heart of leadership and personal accomplishment, the narrative we pen plays a monumental role in the course we tread. This realization anchors the essence of cultivating a growth mindset, a pivotal habit for leadership. Tony Robbins' wisdom encapsulates this: the stories we etch in our psyche either tether us to complacency or propel us into profound success.

A growth mindset isn't a mere motto; it's a transformative lens through which we perceive ourselves and our capabilities. It's understanding that our abilities aren't static; they are ever-evolving. Like a gardener nurturing a plant, a growth mindset insists that with care, persistence, and the right environment, our potential can blossom beyond preconceived bounds.

Think of it as a dance with the infinite possibilities that life presents. It's about silencing that inner voice of doubt and embracing the potent belief that, with resilience and continual learning, barriers become paths forward. The dialogue shifts from "I can't" to "I can learn and improve."

Imagine an entrepreneur with this mindset. They see failures not as dead ends but as invaluable lessons directing their path forward. Such a mindset doesn't insulate one from difficulties; instead, it reframes them. Challenges morph into arenas to showcase grit, tenacity, and an indomitable spirit. It becomes less about setbacks and more about comebacks.

Robbins' words serve as a beacon. By reshaping our inner narratives, we unchain our potential, stepping into an expansive world of opportunities. As the captains of our journey, every thought and action we undertake steers our story toward growth, empowerment, and unparalleled potential.

As you adopt a growth mindset, you realize you hold the power to recraft your story. In the echelons of leadership, this mindset doesn't just produce leaders; it gives birth to pioneers, innovators, and revolutionaries. Their tales stand as beacons, illuminating the transformative power each of us holds. In the narrative of your leadership journey, let the prevailing theme be one of ceaseless growth, undying resolve, and unwavering conviction in the heights you're destined for.

H A B I T

PRIORITIZE PERSONAL DEVELOPMENT

"The biggest room in the world is the room for improvement."

—Helmut Schmidt

L ife is an intricate dance, and every one of us has the innate ability to evolve and grow. Helmut Schmidt's words serve as a reminder that there's always room to better ourselves. As we delve into the essence of personal development, we're introduced to the infinite journey of self-betterment and transformation.

Imagine a blank canvas, ripe with possibility and ready to be painted with knowledge and self-awareness. Leaders who champion personal development are like artists sketching out their vision for the future. This isn't just a nod to self-improvement; it's an all-in commitment to stretch our intellectual, emotional, and spiritual boundaries.

Personal development is more than a solo quest. It celebrates the boundless potential within each of us. It signifies a relentless drive to acquire new skills, navigate unfamiliar terrains, and deeply understand our innate capabilities. Every effort to refine a skill or grasp a new concept enhances our ability to lead with clarity, insight, and empathy.

Think of personal growth as a seed. It needs sunlight, care, and nourishment to flourish. Similarly, nurturing our potential through reading, mentorship, and self-reflection fuels both our personal and professional evolution. Each stride forward molds us into a more enlightened version of ourselves, ready to tackle what's next.

Embracing personal development also means embracing humility. It's an acknowledgment that learning is a lifelong journey. The beauty lies not just in what we know but in our eagerness to learn what we don't.

History is dotted with leaders who have never settled. They've chipped away at their barriers, much like Michelangelo revealed David from a slab of marble. Their dedication to growth lights the way for others.

In the business world, this commitment reshapes leaders. It spurs innovation, strengthens teamwork, and drives a shared pursuit of excellence. As we delve deeper into this habit, keep in mind that the potential for growth is immeasurable. Every decision to learn and evolve adds another brushstroke to your leadership portrait.

So, as you cultivate this habit, remember that you're in good company. This shared quest for growth has been championed by visionary thinkers throughout history. By adopting this habit, you join a legacy of leaders who've recognized the transformative power of personal development and used it to inspire change on a grand scale.

3

H A B I T

PRACTICE DAILY REFLECTION

"An unexamined life is not worth living."

—Socrates

eadership, with all its challenges and triumphs, thrives on a simple yet transformative practice: daily reflection. Socrates' age-old wisdom urges leaders to understand themselves, signaling the start of the "Practice Daily Reflection" chapter. Through reflection, we don't just navigate our lives better; we rise as more aware and effective leaders.

At its heart, daily reflection means taking a deliberate pause amidst the chaos. It's that quiet moment when we dive deep into our experiences, emotions, and thoughts. Much like a captain uses stars to sail through darkness, reflective leaders use insights from their introspections to illuminate their path.

In our fast-paced world, pausing might seem counterproductive. But reflection is essential—it's our compass, guiding us to evaluate our actions, learn from our mistakes, and cherish our successes. Each reflective moment offers a clearer understanding of our journey, pushing us to be better.

Think of your mind as a garden. A mindful gardener nurtures their plants, ensuring they flourish. Similarly, leaders who reflect daily tend to the garden of their minds. They allow seeds of clarity and empathy to grow, letting insights flower and shape their actions.

Reflection isn't just about being alone with your thoughts; it's a conversation with yourself. It's about understanding your motives, dreams, and fears. True leadership is as much about understanding yourself as it is about understanding others.

In business, leaders who make reflection a priority are not just reacting; they're strategizing and moving forward with purpose and authenticity. Their dedication to understanding themselves makes them role models, inspiring others to reflect and grow as well.

So, as you cultivate the habit of daily reflection, know that every introspective moment is a step towards personal growth. In the stillness, you'll find answers, solutions, and revelations that could easily be missed in the noise of everyday life. This journey within not only elevates your leadership but also showcases the profound impact of looking inward.

As you explore the depths of daily reflection, approach your inner world with an open mind and heart. It's through this inward journey that you'll uncover invaluable insights, refining your leadership and guiding you to greater heights.

HABIT

EMBRACE RESILIENCE

> *"Success is not final, failure is not fatal: It is the*
> *courage to continue that counts."*
>
> —Winston Churchill

Leadership is a journey marked by peaks and valleys. Churchill's wisdom reminds us of a golden principle intrinsic to the finest leaders: resilience. This habit doesn't just help us endure challenges; it transforms obstacles into avenues for growth and learning, shaping us into more impactful and steadfast leaders.

Resilience is the bedrock upon which great leaders stand. It's the inner strength that shields against life's whirlwinds, helping us stand tall amidst adversity. Just as an oak tree remains unyielding in the fiercest storms, resilient leaders have a deep-rooted belief in their ability to confront and conquer challenges.

Imagine the phoenix rising anew from its ashes, embodying rebirth and perseverance. Similarly, resilience allows us to rebound from setbacks, viewing failures not as the end but as valuable lessons, redefining our paths to success.

True resilience doesn't stem from avoiding setbacks but from our reaction to them. It's about harnessing failures as lessons and converting them into fuel for our journey ahead. Success isn't the endpoint; it's merely a chapter in our ongoing saga. It's our relentless spirit that carves out our legacy.

Yet resilience isn't a solitary journey. It's interwoven with connections and community. In challenging times, resilient leaders lean on mentors, peers, and teams for advice and encouragement. This support network amplifies our strength, reminding us of the collective resilience we share.

In the business world, leaders embodying resilience inspire teams to navigate fluctuations with agility and poise. By showcasing determination, they cultivate an environment of adaptability and innovation, guiding their organizations to flourish even in uncertain times.

As you delve into the habit of resilience, view challenges as growth opportunities. Every trial is a chance to showcase your grit, to rise, and to evolve into a more formidable leader. By navigating these challenges, you etch your legacy—a testament to the unwavering power of resilience.

Arm yourself with courage, determination, and the conviction that every hurdle can be transformed into another path forward. Echoing Churchill, may you convert every setback into a launchpad, carving a path of unwavering leadership and proving the boundless strength of the human spirit.

H A B I T

MASTER TIME MANAGEMENT

"You may delay, but time will not."

—Benjamin Franklin

Time is the very fabric of our existence. It turns fleeting moments into cherished memories, propels dreams into achievements, and threads aspirations into realities. Benjamin Franklin's wise words remind us that time is unyielding, pressing forward regardless of our wishes or actions. True mastery of time isn't merely about staying punctual; it's about directing our days with purpose, clarity, and an undying pursuit of excellence.

Time management transcends skill—it's an art form. It's the transformation of fleeting seconds and minutes into impactful, deliberate actions. Think of it as sculpting, where every chunk of time chiseled away reveals a clearer reflection of our values, ambitions, and aspirations.

Time is our most precious currency, spent in exchange for experiences, growth, and milestones. Effective leaders, much like prudent investors, manage their time to yield the highest returns, focusing on activities that align with their overarching vision. Every decision in managing time paints a stroke on the vast canvas of their legacy.

The essence of time management isn't to wrestle control over time—an impossible feat—but to effectively steer our actions within its confines. It's about setting a course through life's unpredictable currents with foresight and strategy. Adept leaders recognize that time, once passed, is irretrievable. So, they invest it judiciously, ensuring their actions resonate with their goals.

Instead of clinging to strict schedules, mastering time requires adaptability. Astute leaders grasp the ebb and flow of life, making adjustments when necessary. They employ tools and strategies to find a balance between work, relaxation, and personal development.

In the professional world, leaders who excel in time management don't just boost efficiency; they craft a culture where teams can innovate and excel. Their approach doesn't just streamline tasks—it fosters discipline, accountability, and growth.

Embracing this mastery of time nudges you to view each day as a blank canvas, one you can fill with intention and vision. By harnessing time, leaders compose a journey brimming with purposeful experiences. So, as you delve into the rhythm of managing time, let each moment be filled with clarity and conviction. In doing so, you become more than just efficient—you become a visionary leader who leaves a lasting mark on the annals of time.

Anchoring the Habits of Self-Mastery

Closing the chapter on Self-Mastery, we realize a pivotal insight: the most transformative leadership journeys commence from within. This chapter has been our gateway into introspection, fostering self-awareness, and laying the cornerstone for impactful leadership ahead.

We've embarked on a journey through the terrains of self-discovery, the essence of discipline, the resilience that shapes us, and the intricate dance with time. Embracing a growth mindset, cherishing personal development, and understanding the power of reflection have been our companions. In this process, we've learned that true success lies not just in the peaks we conquer but in the depths we navigate and the wisdom we acquire.

Guided by luminaries like Socrates, Winston Churchill, and Helmut Schmidt, we've been reminded of our potential and the transformative impact we can have—not just on our personal narratives but on those whose lives we touch.

True self-mastery isn't a milestone to be reached but an ever-evolving journey. It's where our strongest attributes coalesce with our vulnerabilities, and genuine self-awareness becomes a beacon for change. This journey asserts that exemplary leadership is born from the inner odyssey, demanding our persistent growth, adaptation, and the shedding of barriers that hinder our genuine selves.

As we transition to the subsequent chapters, the essence of self-mastery should be our guiding light, leading us through the multifaceted aspects of leadership. Remember, akin to a sculptor shaping a masterpiece, we wield the power to design our destinies and inspire those we lead.

May the ethos of self-mastery inform our decisions with clarity, purpose, and authenticity. Let it consistently remind us that to truly lead others, we must first be the captains of our souls—a humbling and empowering task. With self-mastery, we champion our potential, safeguard our growth, and pave the way for a legacy that stands resilient against time—a testament to the human spirit and its boundless possibilities.

As we proceed, our narrative will encompass the nuances of effective communication, the spirit of collaboration, and the essence of fostering a stimulating life. We'll unravel the layers of emotional intelligence and delve into visionary leadership. Yet, throughout this exploration, may we always recall that at its core, leadership thrives on the pulse of self-mastery—a continual reminder that true leadership means leading oneself with grace, insight, and intentionality.

CHAPTER 2

Communication and Collaboration

INTRODUCTION
The Art of Connection

Business is a confluence of ideas, goals, and strategies. In this intricate dance, the twin pillars of communication and collaboration rise as foundational elements. The most visionary leaders are masterful communicators, crafting a rich network of human connections, wielding words and actions that touch hearts, stimulating minds, and shaping futures.

In this chapter, we recognize the quintessential truths driving the monumental power of both communication and collaboration. In our digitally saturated age, the beauty of genuine listening stands out—a practice that enables leaders to discern not only what is spoken but also the underlying emotions, connecting on a profound level. Leaders who excel in communication artfully craft their messages, creating ripples of impact that influence and inspire.

Diving into the ethos of Steve Jobs, who believed in loving one's work to achieve greatness, we unearth the core of inspirational communication. It's not mere eloquence, but genuine passion and unwavering conviction. True leaders become beacons, illuminating paths, igniting enthusiasm, and drawing out the best in everyone.

However, communication isn't an island. It's the bridge to meaningful collaboration, where diverse talents unite, birthing innovations often beyond singular thought. Drawing wisdom from Tony Hsieh's perspective on culture as branding, we understand that collaboration seeps deep, defining the very soul of organizations. Leaders who foster open, inclusive, and transparent cultures aren't just building teams but nurturing communities bound by shared visions and dreams.

True collaboration is like a well-composed symphony—each member plays their part, contributing to a harmonious masterpiece. Visionary leaders, like skilled conductors, weave together individual strengths, creating a resonant harmony that is truly transformative.

In the business landscape, leaders adept in both communication and collaboration emerge as catalysts. They craft spaces where creativity soars, relationships deepen, and novel ideas are celebrated. Through their guidance, teams function cohesively and resonate with a shared purpose, shattering conventions and pioneering change.

Keep in mind that communication and collaboration aren't just tactics; they're the heartbeat of enriched leadership. They equip us to overcome challenges, celebrate diversity, and co-envision futures that leave enduring legacies. Within these pages, each insight, each narrative, and each guideline beckons you—inviting you to embrace the mesmerizing dance of connection and collaboration, lighting the way to impactful leadership.

H A B I T

ACTIVE LISTENING

> *"The most important thing in communication is hearing what isn't said."*
>
> —Peter Drucker

Human interactions are similar to a play in a theater, where every word plays its part. And while spoken words have their spotlight, it's often what remains unsaid that carries the true essence of a conversation. Peter Drucker's words resonate with the age-old wisdom emphasizing the significance of delving beyond the surface of communication. Active listening is not just a habit; it's a bridge leading to deeper understanding, empathy, and genuine connection.

At its heart, active listening isn't merely about being silent when someone speaks. It's a deliberate effort to tune into the undercurrents of a conversation, to sense the emotions and intentions not overtly expressed. It's akin to an artist deeply observing the myriad hues before them, discerning shades that are often overlooked. Leaders who practice active listening are not just hearing; they're deeply understanding the unsaid.

Imagine a treasure chest, securely locked yet brimming with hidden gems. Just as an explorer finds treasure concealed beneath, adept listeners discover wealth in silent moments, gestures, and pauses. These unspoken cues often say more than a barrage of words. Active listeners tune into these, transcending mere conversations to foster genuine relationships.

Active listening goes hand-in-hand with empathy. It's about truly stepping into another's world, feeling their joys, and understanding their challenges. Maya Angelou's words highlight this beautifully: "I've learned that people will forget what you said, people will forget what you did, but people will never forget how you made them feel." Through active listening, leaders leave an indelible mark—a legacy of compassion, validation, and respect.

In business, such leaders stand out. They don't merely forge transactions; they build relationships. They ensure that their teams feel acknowledged and valued, fostering an environment conducive to innovation and excellence. This attentive approach ripples throughout an organization, creating a culture where empathy is integral.

For those who aspire to master active listening, every interaction offers an opportunity to delve deeper and truly connect. It's more than just hearing words; it's about sensing emotions, understanding perspectives, and enriching interactions. This habit is your compass, guiding you towards authentic communication and fostering understanding across divides. Remembering Peter Drucker's wisdom can inspire you to elevate your conversations, ensuring you not only lead with effectiveness but also touch lives profoundly.

HABIT

INSPIRE WITH VISION

"The only way to do great work is to love what you do."

—Steve Jobs

Every leader's journey is like a canvas, where ambition and purpose form the brushstrokes of a grand masterpiece. Steve Jobs believed in the transformative power of loving one's work, and through this, he highlighted an essential leadership quality: the ability to inspire through vision. This isn't just about setting goals; it's about lighting the path with passion.

A vision, painted with genuine enthusiasm, transforms from a mere goal into a magnetic force. It drives innovation, determination, and perseverance. Leaders who harness this force don't merely state objectives; they paint vivid pictures of possibilities, crafting stories that resonate with purpose and passion. By doing so, they create an illuminating path, inviting others to walk alongside them toward a shared aspiration.

True vision goes beyond just seeing the future; it's an embodiment of the ideals and values a leader holds dear. Reflecting on Mahatma Gandhi's wisdom, "You must be the change you wish to see in the world," we realize that leaders must personify their vision, becoming a living testament to the future they seek.

Inspiring with a vision charged with passion knows no boundaries. It dares to challenge the status quo and imagine the unimaginable. Leaders with such a vision don't just set benchmarks; they ignite enthusiasm, fostering an environment where challenges become opportunities, driving the collective forward.

In the business landscape, visionary leaders are the bedrock of transformative cultures. They inspire teams to think beyond the ordinary, to challenge norms, and to embrace innovation with zest. Their fervor creates ripples, turning the spark of an idea into a blazing trail of creativity and achievement.

If you wish to embrace this habit, recognize that your passion is the wind beneath your vision's wings. Your actions, decisions, and words add depth to your vision, and by fueling it with passion, you not only light your path but inspire others to discover their potential.

In your quest to inspire with vision, let your enthusiasm be the guiding star. Commit to crafting a compelling narrative, one that sings with purpose and echoes with authenticity. In the words of Steve Jobs, it's not just about doing great work but also loving it. And when you truly love your vision, you inspire others to journey alongside you toward unparalleled greatness.

H A B I T

FOSTER A CULTURE OF OPENNESS

> *"Your culture is your brand."*
>
> —Tony Hsieh

Within the architecture of organizations, culture stands as the cornerstone, binding values, shaping relationships, and nurturing aspirations. Tony Hsieh's sentiment underscores a truth: culture is not just an abstract concept; it's the very heartbeat of a brand. And at the forefront of thriving cultures is the essence of openness—a commitment to transparency, honesty, and inclusivity that allows for unmatched growth.

Culture is the silent yet formidable force steering an organization's ship. It's not just a set of rules or guidelines; it's the shared ethos that propels an organization forward. To cultivate a culture of openness, one must ensure that every voice within the organization feels valued and that every idea has the space to grow. Leaders championing this habit ensure that protection and space for growth.

Authenticity is vital in an open culture. It's about providing an atmosphere where individuals are encouraged to be genuine, to share their insights without fear, and to collaborate freely. Like a well-conducted orchestra, a culture that values diverse voices creates harmonious melodies, driving the organization to a collective vision.

In such a culture, ideas are revered treasures. It's a space where discussions are stimulated, feedback is welcomed, and innovation is organic. Leaders who champion this understand that growth isn't just about scaling heights; it's about expanding horizons. By promoting openness, they build bridges of understanding, foster innovation, and turn challenges into collaborative opportunities.

Think of an organization's culture as its reflection, capturing its essence, values, and aspirations. Leaders who nurture a culture of openness are shaping this reflection, crafting a narrative that becomes the brand's identity. This brand transcends mere logos—it's a beacon of the values the organization stands for.

In today's dynamic business landscape, leaders who emphasize openness are trailblazers. They establish spaces that promote adaptability, resilience, and proactive thinking. Their influence fosters a workplace that isn't just a hub for tasks but a melting pot of creativity and collaboration, where teams don't just function—they thrive.

As you embark on the journey of fostering a culture of openness, remember that each interaction, decision, and initiative you take molds the very essence of your organization. Your commitment to openness doesn't just benefit the present; it lays the foundation for a promising future. By embracing this habit, you not only create a conducive environment for growth but also etch a lasting brand legacy.

In your pursuit to nurture a culture of openness, champion transparency, celebrate diversity, and let collaboration be your organization's anthem. In this spirit of openness, you'll discover that your brand isn't just about what you offer—it's about who you are and the values you stand for.

H A B I T

EMPOWER OTHERS

"Great leaders are willing to sacrifice their own interests for the good of the group."

—John C. Maxwell

The strength of a group emanates from the collective brilliance of its individuals. As John C. Maxwell explains, it's through the genuine empowerment of others that great leadership truly takes shape. Exploring the talent empowering others, we unearth a habit that's more than just facilitating growth—it's about forging leaders from within, letting them realize their latent potential, and steering them towards collective brilliance.

Leadership is not just about guiding but also about enabling. Great leaders don't just direct; they mold, shape, and foster. The emphasis shifts from mere task completion to holistic development. Leaders who champion this habit understand that their role transcends managerial duties—it's about identifying potential, nurturing it, and letting it shine.

The spirit of empowerment stems from a profound place of selflessness—a recognition that the collective triumphs over individual accolades. Much like a maestro leading an orchestra, these leaders don't seek the spotlight; instead, they focus on harmonizing individual strengths into a cohesive melody. Their success is measured not in their achievements but in the successes of those they empower.

It isn't about giving away power but multiplying it. It's an understanding that when individuals rise, they lift the entire group. Think of it as a chain reaction: the entire chain becomes more robust when one link is strengthened. By empowering an individual, leaders ignite a domino effect, where each empowered member uplifts others.

Empowerment takes on a pivotal role in business. Leaders who engrain this practice into their ethos transform organizations from hierarchical establishments to flat, dynamic ecosystems of empowerment. Hierarchies blur, collaboration becomes organic, and everyone becomes a stakeholder in the company's success. Such an environment not only accelerates innovation but also fosters a deep sense of belonging and purpose.

As you adopt the habit of empowering others, always remember that the echoes of your actions will resonate far and wide. Every seed of empowerment you plant today will grow into a forest of leaders tomorrow. By elevating others, you amplify their potential and engrave a lasting legacy—a legacy where leadership is shared, celebrated, and multiplied.

Treading the path of empowerment, let John C. Maxwell's wisdom be your compass. May your endeavors not be about amassing power but about distributing it. And in this journey, may you not just cultivate leaders but also pioneer a culture of collective brilliance where every individual realizes their potential and shines in unison. For in the genuine empowerment of others lies the epitome of leadership—a leadership that's not about reaching the pinnacle alone but about ensuring everyone summits together.

10

H A B I T

CULTIVATE EMOTIONAL INTELLIGENCE

"People don't care how much you know until they know how much you care."

—Theodore Roosevelt

In leadership, a vital cornerstone that is often overlooked is emotional intelligence (EI). More than just an aptitude, EI encapsulates the heart and soul of genuine leadership. Theodore Roosevelt's poignant words remind us that before we influence or guide, we must first deeply connect. Delving into emotional intelligence, we find not just a habit but a beacon that illuminates the path to authentic and compassionate leadership.

To understand emotional intelligence is to grasp the essence of the human spirit. It's not merely about identifying emotions but about comprehending their depth and navigating them gracefully. Like a masterful maestro, leaders with high EI are attuned to the subtle symphonies of emotions, discerning the crescendos from the diminuendos. They're not just in tune with others but also harmonize their own internal orchestra, leading with both heart and mind.

Emotional intelligence's magic lies in its duality—introspection paired with outward empathy. It's about possessing a keen sense of self-awareness, recognizing one's strengths, vulnerabilities, and emotional triggers, and equally discerning the emotional landscapes of others. Leaders who harness this potent combination become formidable forces of positive influence, turning challenges into opportunities for connection and growth.

Imagine leadership as a bridge connecting diverse landscapes and terrains. Emotional intelligence becomes the foundation of this bridge, ensuring it's sturdy, resilient, and dependable. Leaders who prioritize EI don't just build bridges; they fortify them, ensuring that the connections they forge withstand the test of time, challenges, and uncertainties.

In business, emotional intelligence evolves from being an asset to a necessity. In a world driven by metrics and data, EI reintroduces the irreplaceable human touch. Leaders endowed with high emotional intelligence are the architects of corporate cultures where trust, empathy, and understanding become cornerstones. They foster environments where innovation isn't just welcomed but is born from a place of genuine collaboration and shared vision.

EI, leadership transforms from a role into a heartfelt commitment—one where success is measured not just in milestones but in the depth of connections and the positive impact created.

Through emotional intelligence, we can be remembered for our direction, depth, empathy, and authentic connections. True leadership transcends titles—it resonates in the hearts of those we touch, influence, and inspire.

Anchoring the Habits of Communication and Collaboration

The values of collaboration and communication have enriched the concept of leadership throughout Chapter 2. As we journeyed through these habits, we navigated the intricate landscape of relationships, influence, and collective purpose.

We began with the gentle art of active listening, discovering that to truly understand, one must immerse themselves in the profound depths of silence and empathy. Guided by Peter Drucker's insights, we recognized that genuine communication extends far beyond spoken words—it envelops feelings, perceptions, and silent cries for validation.

Our exploration led us to the heart of inspiration. With Steve Jobs as our beacon, we uncovered the transformative power of passion—how it not only drives individual brilliance but also kindles the sparks in others. As leaders, when we radiate our passion, we light a pathway for others to discover and embrace their own.

The canvas of our leadership journey was further enriched by the vibrant colors of openness and transparency. Drawing wisdom from Tony Hsieh's philosophy, we understood that a culture's essence is its soul, its brand. An open culture doesn't just foster creativity; it becomes a crucible where trust, authenticity, and innovation meld seamlessly.

Our pathway was illuminated by the guiding light of empowerment, reminding us that true leadership lies in uplifting others. Inspired by John C. Maxwell, we were called to a higher purpose—a commitment to place the collective's needs and aspirations above our own, nurturing growth, potential, and shared success.

And as our journey reached its zenith, we embraced the profound concept of emotional intelligence. Theodore Roosevelt's wisdom served as a poignant reminder that leadership, at its core, is a testament to human connection. To lead is to care, to understand, and to connect authentically.

In conclusion, as we stand at the precipice of this chapter, gazing back at the landscape we've traversed, a beautiful mosaic emerges. The mosaic of communication and collaboration, crafted from the tiles of active listening, inspiration, openness, empowerment, and emotional intelligence, paints a vivid picture of what leadership truly entails. It's a journey of the heart as much as the mind, where every interaction, decision, and gesture is an opportunity to forge bonds and amplify our collective impact.

May we stride forward, carrying these invaluable lessons as the compass of our leadership voyage. As we continue to sculpt our leadership narrative, let it be infused with the spirit of collaboration, the power of authentic connection, and the timeless essence of genuine care. In this intricate dance of leadership, may we always be guided by the harmony of hearts and minds, amplifying our impact and forging bonds that echo through eternity.

CHAPTER 3

Decision-Making and Problem-Solving

Navigating the Seas of Clarity and Resolution

Leadership, at its core, is an expedition—a journey of choices, challenges, and opportunities. The path, often unpaved, unfolds through the decisions we make and the problems we solve. Chapter 3, "Decision-Making and Problem-Solving," promises to be a beacon, guiding leaders through the intricate mazes that arise in their leadership journey.

Every decision leaves a mark on the canvas of our leadership narrative. These decisions, whether monumental or seemingly trivial, build upon one another, creating the mosaic of our impact and influence. Within the folds of this chapter, we'll delve into the depths of decision-making, unraveling its nuances and dissecting its layers to discern the essence of effective and ethical choices.

Hand in hand with decision-making is the art of problem-solving. Every leader, no matter how visionary or strategic, encounters challenges. But it's not the presence of these challenges that defines leadership; it's the approach to them. Problems, seen through a refined lens, transform into opportunities—chances to innovate, reimagine, and evolve. We will decode the alchemy of turning adversities into advantages, setting the stage for innovative solutions and breakthrough moments.

Both decision-making and problem-solving, though distinct in their nature, intertwine in the dance of leadership. They reflect a leader's philosophy, resilience, and adaptability. This chapter, therefore, is more than just a theoretical exploration; it's a deep dive into the soul of leadership, providing a compass for navigating its complex terrain.

We will venture into the territories of strategic thinking, ethical considerations, collaborative methodologies, and the delicate balance between intuition and logic. Along the way, we will glean insights from renowned leaders by dissecting their decision-making processes and problem-solving methodologies, providing a holistic understanding that merges theory with practice.

As you turn the pages of Chapter 3, envision it as a voyage—one that empowers you to navigate the unpredictable waters of leadership with a fortified mindset and sharpened skills. With every section, you'll be better equipped to make decisions that resonate with purpose and solve problems with creativity and insight.

May this chapter serve as a guiding star, illuminating the path of every leader who seeks to make impactful decisions and craft ingenious solutions. Let's embark on this enlightening journey, charting a course that melds purpose with action and vision with execution.

H A B I T

EMBRACE ACCOUNTABILITY

"The price of greatness is responsibility."

—Winston Churchill

As leaders, our actions have profound implications, and our decisions carve paths. At the heart of truly great leadership is a deep-seated sense of accountability. This sentiment, captured by Winston Churchill, emphasizes that true greatness stems from embracing responsibility wholeheartedly. By diving into the habit of "Embrace Accountability," we learn that this isn't just about fulfilling obligations—it's about fully owning our actions, whether they lead to success or setbacks, and guiding our journey with intention.

Accountability isn't just a buzzword; it's the backbone of genuine trust and integrity. Think of it as a foundational pillar, stabilizing and strengthening everything built upon it. Leaders who wholeheartedly adopt accountability don't just hold themselves to high standards; they foster trustworthiness, a crucial element in effective leadership.

Being accountable means recognizing both our triumphs and our missteps. It's easy to claim victories, but true leaders also admit and learn from their errors. This creates an atmosphere of honesty, allowing for genuine growth and collaboration.

Moreover, accountability paves the way for improvement. Rather than shying away from mistakes, exemplary leaders examine them, seeking to understand, learn, and adapt. In this context, every setback offers a lesson; every challenge is an opportunity.

Imagine a captain navigating through stormy seas. Those who hold themselves accountable don't abandon ship at the first sign of trouble. They lead, providing direction and assurance, ensuring the journey continues confidently despite hurdles.

In business, such leaders build resilient and adaptable teams. They set the tone, motivating everyone to take charge of their roles. This creates an environment where responsibility is empowered, sparking a unified drive towards excellence.

So, as you journey through leadership, remember: every decision and every step you take will be built into your legacy. Owning up to your choices, both good and bad, establishes a legacy of trust and becomes an inspiration to others. Embracing accountability not only acknowledges the triumphs but also celebrates the journey of growth and learning.

In your pursuit of accountability, let Churchill's words be your guiding light. Stand tall on the pillars of responsibility and integrity, shaping a legacy that champions both achievement and the invaluable lessons that come with growth.

H A B I T

DATA-DRIVEN DECISION-MAKING

"In God we trust; all others must bring data."

—W. Edwards Deming

To be successful leaders, we must rely on data-driven insights as a trusted compass. W. Edwards Deming's iconic statement emphasizes the weight and value of basing decisions on hard evidence. In the world of "Data-Driven Decision-Making," we move beyond mere intuition, leveraging concrete data to guide our leadership path.

Data isn't just a series of numbers. Think of it as a story told through patterns and trends, offering insights that, when interpreted correctly, become invaluable guidance. Just as an architect wouldn't build without a plan, savvy leaders use data to lay the foundation for their strategies, turning raw numbers into actionable insights.

It's essential to understand that being data-driven isn't just for analysts. Leaders at all levels can bolster their decisions with evidence. Tapping into data means bypassing biases and assumptions and anchoring decisions in the reality of the situation.

Furthermore, data opens the door to innovation. Leaders who embrace data can spot hidden opportunities, challenge norms, and push boundaries. It's like mining for diamonds; by delving deep, you unearth gems of insight that can spark transformative change.

Imagine using a detailed map on an unfamiliar journey. That's what data-driven leaders offer their teams: a detailed guide through the challenges and complexities of the business landscape. With data in hand, they chart courses that are not only informed but also tailored to the organization's objectives.

Leaders who prioritize data in their approach foster agility and competitiveness. By championing evidence-based strategies, they enable organizations to evolve and excel in today's dynamic world. This creates a culture where data isn't just a tool—it's an integral part of the organizational mindset.

So, as you incorporate data-driven decision-making into your leadership, consider each piece of data as a puzzle piece. Together, these pieces form a comprehensive picture, enabling informed choices that enrich your leadership journey. Harnessing data means championing accuracy and clarity in a world often riddled with ambiguity.

As you go deeper into this data-driven world, channel the essence of Deming's words. Let data be your guiding star, directing you towards informed, impactful decisions. By committing to this approach, you're not just advancing your organization; you're redefining leadership for the modern era.

H A B I T

SEEK DIVERSE PERSPECTIVES

"Strength lies in differences, not in similarities."

—Stephen R. Covey

In leadership's vast landscape, where challenges become opportunities and different viewpoints sculpt the outcome, valuing diverse perspectives is like cherishing a cache of invaluable gems. Stephen R. Covey's words remind us that leadership is enriched when we open ourselves to the myriad of experiences that surround us. "Seek Diverse Perspectives" isn't just a call for variety—it's an invitation to open our minds, allowing varied insights to mold our strategies and decisions.

Diversity isn't merely a mix of voices; it's the confluence of cultures, experiences, and perspectives that come together to paint a richer picture. Imagine an artist, with a palette of myriad colors, creating a masterpiece. That's what leaders do when they invite diverse opinions—they paint solutions and strategies that are vibrant, nuanced, and holistic. In this, they become stewards of adaptability and innovation.

Central to this habit is understanding that genuine progress happens when we step out of our comfort zones and immerse ourselves in the richness of diverse thoughts. Much like the facets of a diamond contribute to its brilliance, a leader's decisions shine when illuminated by various viewpoints. By welcoming these perspectives, leaders foster an ecosystem where innovation thrives naturally.

Valuing diverse perspectives is also an exercise in empathy. It's about truly listening to others, understanding their experiences, and recognizing the value they bring. In doing so, leaders cultivate environments of belonging where every voice is cherished.

Think of leadership as crafting a mosaic. Each piece, different and unique, comes together to depict a story more significant than its individual parts. Leaders who value diversity are like these mosaic artists, piecing together a beautiful narrative of collective wisdom.

In the business world, such leaders are pivotal for fostering innovation and adaptability. They see potential where others see differences, and solutions where others see problems. This mindset, this culture, transcends the confines of an office—it fosters a world where diversity is harnessed for its immense potential.

As you adopt this habit, remember: every voice you listen to and every perspective you consider paints your leadership journey in richer colors. By valuing these varied insights, you champion inclusivity and innovation. You not only elevate your leadership but also craft a world where differences are both celebrated and embraced.

So, as you walk this path of valuing diverse perspectives, take to heart Stephen R. Covey's wisdom. In seeking and valuing diverse perspectives, you stand as a leader who listens, understands, and champions the collective strength found in our differences.

HABIT

ANALYZE RISK AND REWARD

"The biggest risk is not taking any risk."

—Mark Zuckerberg

Mastering the ability to analyze risk and reward is an invaluable skill as a leader. The art of calculated risk-taking can be the catalyst for unparalleled growth and groundbreaking achievements. Delving into "Analyze Risk and Reward," we undertake a voyage that breaks away from the anchors of fear—it is a pursuit to leverage risks and rewards to become visionary leadership.

Risks should never be gambled on or taken blindly. Risks are insightful explorations based on a careful assessment of the landscape. In the same way a sailor uses stars for navigation, adept leaders utilize their knowledge, intuition, and experience to weigh the pros and cons before plunging into decisions. In doing so, they masterfully steer their ship through the choppy waters of uncertainty, tapping into opportunities that might daunt the less prepared.

Central to this habit is understanding that risk and reward are two sides of the same coin. Like a mountaineer pushing for the peak despite challenges, leaders know that the most significant rewards often come from meticulously calculated risks. Embracing this ethos, they foster a culture where growth is fueled by an adventurous spirit grounded in strategy.

Delving into risk and reward requires a visionary lens—seeing beyond the immediacy and envisioning what could be. Leaders adept in this area are the cartographers of the future, charting courses that meld potential gains with informed caution. Their approach continually redefines boundaries and challenges the limits of possibility.

Imagine a tightrope walker poised perfectly between audacity and caution. Such is the demeanor of leaders proficient in analyzing risk and reward. Their journey is a balancing act, always on the edge but consistently grounded by knowledge, intuition, and a clear-eyed vision of the potential fallout.

Leaders who adeptly balance risk and reward sow seeds of innovation and expansion. By championing well-informed risk-taking, they inject dynamism into the organizational ethos, pushing teams to stretch their imagination and redefine their limits. Their influence permeates entire sectors, shaping a milieu where audacious decisions are fueled by understanding and determination.

As you habitually analyze risk and reward, remember: every choice and every venture should only be taken after careful analysis. By mastering this balance, you champion progress and embody transformation, carving pathways to futures previously deemed unattainable.

By mastering the art of analyzing risk and reward, you create an enduring legacy—one of visionary decisions, groundbreaking innovations, and leadership that both inspires and transforms.

15
H A B I T

ADAPTABILITY AND FLEXIBILITY

> *"It's not the strongest of the species that survive, nor the most intelligent, but the one most responsive to change."*
>
> —Charles Darwin

Adaptability and flexibility are what leaders need to practice most. Echoing Charles Darwin's wisdom, we're reminded that thriving isn't about resisting change but embracing its rhythm. Within "Adaptability and Flexibility," we embark on a journey that breaks rigid confines—a pledge to fluidity, agility, and evolving in a changing world.

Adaptability isn't just reacting; it's anticipating—an active embrace of change as a gateway to potential. Like a reed swaying yet unbroken, leaders in adaptability mold their visions to stay relevant. Through this agility, they stand as sentinels of resilience, priming teams for the foreseeable and unforeseeable.

Change isn't an interruption; it's life's pulse. Leaders who weave adaptability grasp that every twist holds the promise of insight. By celebrating this rhythm, they foster cultures where change isn't a challenge but a catalyst for innovation.

The journey of adaptability and flexibility is perpetual reinvention—a vow to stay curious, challenge norms, and confront the unknown un-flinchingly. Leaders like these craft legacies rooted not in adapting to change but in pioneering it. Their ethos inspires teams to see transformation as a journey to explore new heights.

Imagine a sailboat swaying with capricious winds yet steadfastly steering. Leaders who embrace adaptability are like seasoned sailors, harnessing change to propel forward. They adjust their sails as needed, keeping sight of their destination. Their leadership is unwavering yet seamlessly attuned to shifting tides.

In business, leaders who embrace adaptability cultivate legacies of inventive perseverance. By openly welcoming change, they infuse enterprises with a rejuvenating spirit, motivating collaborators to shape change. Their influence nurtures cultures where adaptability guides, nurtures, and propels progress.

As you internalize adaptability, remember that every embrace of change enriches your leadership narrative. By championing adaptability and flexibility, you become a conductor of metamorphosis—a leader who thrives amid change, orchestrating its transformative melody.

As you journey, draw strength from Darwin's insight. Let your dedication shape you into a beacon—a leader who harnesses change's ebb and flow, molding them into harmonies of growth. By embodying adaptability and flexibility, you carve a legacy of fluidity, tenacity, and belief in the power of the ever-changing winds.

Anchoring the Habits of Decision-Making and Problem-Solving

As Chapter 3, "Decision-Making and Problem-Solving," draws to a close, we stand on the brink of transformation. Here, we've explored the nuances of choices, the transition from challenges to solutions, and the intricate dance of managing complexity in leadership.

This chapter took us on a voyage. We navigated self-mastery, celebrated the unison of communication and collaboration, and emphasized the importance of data-driven insights. Along the way, we discovered that leadership isn't just about authority; it's an art. It's where strategy, empathy, and bravery converge.

Tony Robbins' wisdom emphasized the role of self-awareness. By understanding and mastering our stories, we pave the way for better choices. This isn't just about control; it's about creating a meaningful narrative for our lives.

The nuances of communication and collaboration served as our beacon. We learned the value of listening actively, embracing diverse perspectives, and building a shared vision. These are not just skills; they are the bedrock of effective leadership.

In our data-driven era, the chapter highlighted how insights guide our decisions. Facts and figures are more than numbers; they're the tools that offer clarity in a world brimming with choices.

The chapter's end underscored adaptability and flexibility as essentials. In the unpredictable seas of change, these qualities are our anchors, ensuring we remain agile and resilient.

However, the magic lies not just in these individual lessons but in their amalgamation. Leadership isn't a solitary journey. It's collaborative, innovative, and timeless. Every habit we've touched upon adds to the grand mosaic of effective leadership, underlined by authenticity, foresight, and growth.

As we move into the next chapter, let's remember these insights not just as theories but as guiding principles. They remind us that leadership is more than a role—it's a responsibility. By refining our decision-making and problem-solving skills, we journey from mere managers to true leaders. In this evolution, we find clarity, inspire innovation, and lead change, crafting a legacy marked by genuine impact, wisdom, and excellence.

CHAPTER 4

Leadership and Team Building

Forging Bonds, Inspiring Greatness

Leadership and team building play a pivotal role in the world of organizational dynamics. These elements, like the notes in a musical symphony, come together in harmony to produce a masterpiece. As we read through Chapter 4, we'll explore the essence of leadership and the magic of building cohesive teams.

True leadership extends beyond a title; it's about influence. It's about setting a direction, motivating, and bringing people along for the journey. In this chapter, we'll venture into what makes a leader effective and how one can inspire and empower individuals to achieve collective success.

Yet, leadership doesn't stand alone. It's interwoven with the art of team-building. A strong leader is only as successful as the team behind them. We'll uncover the nuances of building a team where collaboration and communication lead to synergy. Imagine a conductor leading an orchestra. Each musician plays a different instrument, yet they come together to produce a harmonious tune. Similarly, effective team building is about bringing diverse talents together, united under a common vision.

Throughout this chapter, we'll explore the importance of clear communication, building trust, and setting a vision that resonates with everyone.

We'll learn how cultivating diversity can be a game-changer and how creating an environment of growth leads to innovation.

Great leaders leave an indelible mark—a legacy. Their influence, combined with that of a cohesive team, can change the trajectory of entire organizations. As we journey through these pages, remember that leadership isn't about dominating; it's about serving and guiding. And team building is more than just grouping individuals together; it's about creating a space where everyone feels valued and works towards a shared goal.

As we develop the habits of a leader who builds great teams, let's embrace the wisdom that leadership is not just about authority; it is about service, vision, and the ability to rally hearts and minds toward a shared purpose. The art of team building includes pivotal aspects that reach far beyond just the business world.

16

H A B I T

LEAD BY EXAMPLE

> *"You don't lead by pointing and telling people some place to go. You lead by going to that place and making a case."*
>
> —Ken Kesey

Actions speak louder than words, and showing what you can do makes you influential. Leading by example is a vital part of being a good leader. At the core of what it means to be a leader who does more than talk, we learn about leading by doing.

Leading by example isn't a mere gesture; it's a transformative force—a ripple emanating from authentic leadership's core. Just as a lighthouse steadfastly guides ships through turbulent waters, leaders who embody this principle serve as beacons of inspiration, steering their teams with unwavering purpose. Through their actions, they become architects of trust—a trust that isn't built solely on rhetoric but rather on the foundation of shared commitment and lived experiences.

A profound understanding lies at the heart of this habit: leadership isn't merely a privilege; it's a responsibility. Leaders who prioritize leading by example recognize that they aren't exempt from the standards they set; instead, they are held to a higher level of accountability. By embracing this accountability, they cultivate a culture where values transcend slogans and become a way of life—an environment where authenticity reigns as the currency of influence.

Leading by example isn't just a journey of actions; it's also a journey of influence, a promise to fight for change not preached from behind but from the front lines of action. Leaders who support this journey know that what they do is more important than what they say. By taking the lead, they tell a story of courage, conviction, and tenacity that inspires their teams to leave their comfort zones and enter uncharted territory.

Business leaders who prioritize leading by example become architects of transformation and accountability. By personifying the principles, they champion, they foster environments where authenticity flourishes and trust evolves into the cornerstone of relationships. Their actions resonate across organizations, nurturing cultures where each individual becomes a steward of purpose and dedication.

As you embrace the habit of leading by doing, remember that each stride you take and each value you embody contributes to a narrative of influence and impact. Every step, each demonstration of dedication, shapes the core of your leadership journey. By leading by doing, you metamorphose into a torchbearer of inspiration—an authenticity and empowerment architect who doesn't articulate a vision but lives it. Through your embodiment, you breathe life into aspirations and craft a legacy of purpose.

As you lead by doing, infuse your path with the spirit of Ken Kesey's wisdom. Through your dedication, you evolve into a leader who doesn't just point the way but walks it, illuminating the trail of inspiration with your deeds. By leading by doing, you leave a legacy of authenticity, trust, and transformative leadership. This legacy guides your own odyssey and sparks unwavering dedication and purpose in those who follow.

H A B I T

DEVELOP THE PERSON

> *"Leadership is not about being in charge. It's about taking care of those in your charge."*
>
> —Simon Sinek

True leadership goes beyond wielding authority; it lies in nurturing, guiding, and elevating those under your wing. Simon Sinek's wisdom touches upon this core essence of leadership, emphasizing the significance of mentorship and genuine concern for others' success. Within the framework of "Develop People," we are invited to see leadership not as a series of commands but as a pledge to help individuals achieve their utmost potential.

To develop others is more than an organizational task—it's a moral duty. It's understanding that leadership isn't just about the role you occupy but also the growth you foster in others. Think of a dedicated gardener who attentively tends to their plants. Similarly, leaders who prioritize human development foster an atmosphere where potential can blossom and individuals can soar. They are not just taskmasters but enablers of transformation beyond professional boundaries.

Central to this is the realization that leadership isn't just a title—it's an opportunity. These leaders don't just issue directives; they unlock the latent power within each individual. They create a culture where mentorship is valued and continuous learning becomes a collective endeavor.

Imagine a sculptor, with each chisel stroke revealing the masterpiece within a raw stone. In the same vein, leaders act as sculptors of human potential, carving out the best in individuals and guiding them to discover their strengths and passions. They are the igniters of innovation, instilling values of perseverance and excellence.

In business, leaders focused on human development lay the foundation for sustainable growth. Investing in individuals creates a pool of talents and insights, driving organizations toward new horizons. Such actions ripple through teams, creating environments where each member thrives and learning is celebrated.

Remember, every moment you spend mentoring or guiding someone is a step towards shaping the future. It's about leaving a lasting impact, one that elevates not only the individual but the collective spirit. Embrace this habit, and you're not just leading but also inspiring, motivating, and making a lasting difference. As you journey through the world of leadership, let Sinek's words be your compass—leading not from a position of power but from a place of genuine care and mentorship.

H A B I T

BUILDING TRUST

"Trust is the glue of life. It's the most essential ingredient in effective communication. It's the foundational principle that holds all relationships."

—Stephen R. Covey

eadership, in all its facets and intricacies, hinges on trust. Stephen R. Covey's perspective encapsulates the importance of trust as the linchpin of impactful leadership. Diving into "Building Trust," we are reminded that leadership is more than just guiding; it's about cultivating bonds rooted in authenticity, transparency, and unwavering reliability.

Trust isn't a mere add-on; it's the foundation. Just as bridges connect two lands, a leader must act as that sturdy bridge, facilitating connections based on mutual respect, shared goals, and faith in each other. Such leaders lay the foundations for united teams, ensuring transactions transform into deep-rooted relationships.

True to this habit's essence, trust isn't built overnight. Successful leaders understand that trust is cultivated through consistent actions, clear communication, and unwavering moral compasses. It's about creating an environment where promises are kept, mistakes are acknowledged, and every action resonates with integrity.

Imagine a sturdy bridge standing tall amidst turbulent waters, providing a safe pathway. Leaders should aim to be this bridge, bridging gaps with the steel of trust and the cement of reliability, ensuring ideas and relationships prosper in a culture of trust.

In the business landscape, trust-oriented leaders pave the way for enduring loyalty. They foster an environment where employees feel valued and understood, promoting a workspace where trust isn't just spoken but lived and breathed. Such trust-centric ecosystems yield genuine collaboration, loyalty, and long-term success.

Embracing trust means honoring commitments, being transparent, and prioritizing reliability. It's about more than just leading—it's about connecting, shaping, and inspiring. As you foster trust, remember that each action and decision lays another brick in your legacy's foundation, defining the kind of leader you become.

Let Stephen R. Covey's words guide you. Aim to be a leader who doesn't just communicate but does so with integrity, fostering bonds that stand the test of time. Building trust means shaping a legacy grounded in authenticity and fostering relationships that don't just exist but thrive.

HABIT

ENCOURAGE INNOVATION

"Innovation distinguishes between a leader and a follower."

—Steve Jobs

The dynamic world of leadership is defined by its constant evolution, where embracing change and fostering creativity become the backbone of progress. Steve Jobs' statement encapsulates the essence of leadership: one that's not content with the status quo but perpetually seeks to redefine it. "Encouraging Innovation" beckons us to an exciting journey beyond the familiar—a quest to nurture imagination, celebrate curiosity, and champion the bold spirit of inventive thinking.

Innovation isn't merely a goal; it's a lifeline. Just as a spark can ignite a mighty blaze, leaders championing innovation light the path to creative discovery. By stoking the flames of curiosity, they drive forward-thinking and shape an era of progressive ideas.

This habit emphasizes that innovation isn't exclusive—it thrives in every individual. By cultivating an environment where every team member feels empowered to think differently, leaders build a realm where curiosity isn't just encouraged; it's the norm.

The journey to foster innovation is as much about embracing failures as it is about celebrating successes. Leaders prioritize environments where taking risks is celebrated and setbacks are learning curves. Such leadership creates spaces where exploration isn't just welcomed; it's essential.

Think of leaders as lighthouses, standing tall amidst uncertainty and providing direction. Their light encourages teams to brave uncharted waters, paving the way for novel ideas and transformative solutions.

In the corporate sphere, these visionary leaders are not just contributors but game-changers. They recognize the value of fresh perspectives, ensuring organizations aren't just participants in the race but, often, the ones leading it. Such leadership not only drives advancement but also shapes the future landscape of industries.

As you venture into fostering innovation, understand that every risk you take and every creative endeavor you support is another step in building a legacy of imaginative leadership. It's about redefining boundaries, enabling transformative thought, and inspiring teams to see beyond the obvious.

Channel the spirit of Steve Jobs as you champion innovation. Let your leadership not just foresee change but be the driving force behind it. Embracing innovation isn't just about personal growth; it's about setting the stage for a future where challenges are met with creativity, ensuring your leadership leaves an enduring impact on the annals of progress.

H A B I T

DELEGATION AND EMPOWERMENT

"The best executive is the one who has sense enough to pick good men to do what he wants done, and self-restraint enough to keep from meddling with them while they do it."

—Theodore Roosevelt

L eadership goes beyond making decisions and outlining strategies. It's a dance of trust where delegation and empowerment set the rhythm that guides teams to excellence. Echoing Theodore Roosevelt, true leadership finds balance in recognizing talent and entrusting it to shine. This chapter explores the territory of trust, where leaders unlock potential and build bridges to collective brilliance.

Delegation is more than splitting tasks; it's a vote of confidence. Like a conductor allowing musicians their solos while guiding the orchestra, leaders grasp that empowerment lets individuals excel in their unique strengths. This approach creates a mosaic of talents, adding value to the whole.

At its core, this habit acknowledges that leadership thrives on collaboration, not isolation. Leaders who value delegation and empowerment understand the power of teamwork over individual skill. This belief fosters an environment where trust prevails and individuals don't just complete tasks; they own them.

Delegating and empowering form a pact of mutual respect. Leaders extend trust, and teams respond with autonomy and purpose. These leaders act as facilitators, ensuring teams have the resources, freedom, and confidence to deliver their best.

Picture a conductor guiding a musical ensemble. Instruments play distinct parts, merging into a harmonious whole. Likewise, leaders who master delegation become conductors of their organizations, channeling individual talents into a symphony of collective brilliance.

In business, these leaders drive efficiency and innovation. By advocating autonomy, they create spaces where inspiration flows, innovation thrives, and shared purpose unites teams. Their actions cultivate cultures where individuals aren't just participants but active contributors.

As you explore delegation and empowerment, remember that each task you delegate and every ounce of trust you give contribute to a legacy of collaborative brilliance. By entrusting and empowering, you become a leader who guides and trusts, propelling teams toward success.

Let Theodore Roosevelt's wisdom be your compass. Strive to be a leader who strategizes, guides, and uplifts. Embracing delegation and empowerment crafts a legacy celebrating trust, respect, and shared victories—a journey defining your leadership while elevating all who share it with you.

Anchoring the Habits of Leadership and Team Building

As we close Chapter 4, we see that the journey of leadership is not a solitary one but a collective endeavor, weaving together the aspirations and talents of many into a cohesive network of shared vision and success.

The chapter illuminated the diverse facets of leadership—from setting the benchmark through personal example to nurturing potential, fostering an ecosystem of trust to igniting the flames of innovation, and entrusting and empowering individuals to be co-creators of the collective journey.

The underlying theme that resonates throughout is the intertwined dance between leadership and team building. A dance where every step, gesture, and decision by the leader sets the team's rhythm, tone, and pace. It emphasizes that leadership is not about the supremacy of one but the elevation of all.

We delved into the essence of leading authentically, where genuineness becomes the bedrock upon which foundations of trust are built. In nurturing talents, we recognized the transformative power of guidance and mentorship and the value of investing in human potential. Trust, as we discovered, is not a given; it is earned, preserved, and deepened through consistent actions and unwavering integrity.

Our foray into innovation was a vivid testament to the fact that true leaders don't just adapt to change; they champion it. They inspire their teams to look beyond the horizon, challenge the status quo, and carve pathways previously unimagined. And in the dance of delegation and empowerment, we were reminded that a leader's true strength lies in their ability to let go, to entrust responsibilities, and to empower their teams to own, act, and excel.

As this chapter comes to a close, it beckons us to reflect, internalize, and act. Recognizing that leadership is more than a title; it's a responsibility, a commitment, and a privilege to inspire, guide, and elevate others. It's about building bridges of understanding, pathways of collaboration, and highways of shared success.

To be a leader is to be a beacon, guiding not just through words but actions, direction, and inspiration. To build a team is to recognize the symphony in diversity, the strength in unity, and the magic that happens when individual aspirations align with collective goals.

As we turn the page, let's carry the profound insights and lessons from this chapter, and add them to our leadership toolkits. Let's strive to be leaders who don't just command respect but earn it, who don't just lead teams but empower them, and whose legacy is not just about personal achievements but the collective successes and dreams realized.

Here's to leadership that unites hearts and guides teams toward unparalleled greatness.

CHAPTER 5

Strategic Thinking and Planning

Illuminating the Path to Organizational Brilliance

I n the dynamic landscape of leadership, where visions are cast, horizons are explored, and destinies are crafted, the art of strategic thinking and planning emerges as a guiding light—a beacon that directs organizations toward their most ambitious goals. As we embark on the voyage through Chapter 5, "Strategic Thinking and Planning," we venture into ideas where foresight melds with action, where innovation meets execution, and where the blueprint of success is drawn with precision and purpose.

Strategic thinking and planning are not mere theoretical constructs; they are the scaffolds upon which the architecture of achievement is erected. Like master architects envisioning a majestic structure, leaders who embrace strategic thinking and planning chart courses that transcend the mundane, offering a framework for growth, sustainability, and the pursuit of excellence. Within this chapter, we delve into the strategies that propel organizations from potential to reality, from aspirations to impactful outcomes.

Strategic thinking is the lens through which leaders perceive opportunities, challenges, and trends. It is the ability to envision a future that goes beyond the immediate horizon, fostering a culture of proactive decision-making and nimble adaptation. Strategic planning, on the other hand, is the compass that guides these visions into reality—a roadmap that delineates the steps, resources, and timelines required to bring aspirations to fruition.

Our exploration through this chapter will navigate vision creation, goal setting, risk assessment, resource allocation, and the seamless fusion of strategy and execution. We will the meaning of strategic leadership—a link that connects insight with action and aligns individual efforts with collective aspirations.

As we journey through the landscapes of strategic thinking and planning, let us heed the wisdom of history's trailblazers and modern visionaries. Let us recognize that every decision we make, every resource we allocate, contributes to a narrative of transformation—a narrative that shapes the trajectory of organizations, influences industries, and leaves an indelible mark on the ever-evolving work of leadership.

Strategic thinking and planning are not confined to boardrooms or executive meetings; they are the pulse of leadership that beats in every decision, every action, and every interaction. As we embrace this chapter, let us embark on a voyage of insight and foresight, of deliberate choices and thoughtful execution. By honing the skills of strategic thinking and planning, we take the helm of our leadership journey, steering toward the shores of innovation, excellence, and the profound impact that only strategic leadership can achieve.

HABIT

SET CLEAR GOALS

> *"You have to set goals that are almost out of reach. If you set a goal that is attainable without much work or thought, you are stuck with something below your true talent and potential."*
>
> —Steve Garvey

Strategic thinking and planning stand out as crucial elements of leadership when learning how to lead and carry over into years of successful development. These concepts act like a guiding star, leading organizations to their highest aspirations. As we journey through Chapter 5, "Strategic Thinking and Planning," we'll explore how foresight becomes action, how innovation blends with execution, and how a clear plan can define the path to success.

Strategic thinking and planning aren't just buzzwords; they form the foundation for genuine achievement. Imagine master architects meticulously planning a grand building. Similarly, leaders, by harnessing strategic thinking and planning, lay out clear paths, pushing boundaries, and setting the stage for growth and excellence. This chapter will shed light on the strategies that take an organization from a mere concept to tangible success.

Strategic thinking allows leaders to spot opportunities, face challenges, and identify trends. It's about looking ahead, beyond the immediate challenges, to shape a proactive and adaptable culture. Meanwhile, strategic planning is the actionable counterpart to this vision. The plan, detailing steps, resources, and timeframes, turns dreams into reality.

This chapter will dive into vision creation, setting goals, evaluating risks, allocating resources, and ensuring that strategy aligns perfectly with execution. We'll discover the essence of strategic leadership, a unique blend of insight and action that harmonizes individual roles with larger organizational goals.

We'll draw inspiration from past pioneers and today's innovators throughout this journey. Every decision and allocated resource plays a pivotal role, contributing to a transformative story that redefines industries and imprints on the legacy of leadership.

Remember, strategic thinking and planning aren't just for the boardroom; they infuse life into every leadership decision and action. As we delve into this chapter, we'll navigate the nuanced worlds of insight and foresight, making choices with care and precision. Embracing strategic thinking and planning, we steer our leadership voyage, navigating towards innovation, excellence, and lasting impact.

22

FOCUS ON THE BIG PICTURE

"The difference between a successful person and others is not a lack of strength, not a lack of knowledge, but rather a lack in will."

—Vince Lombardi

Leadership often confronts a whirlwind of tasks, details, and potential distractions. Amidst this, the power of focusing on the big picture stands as a beacon. Vince Lombardi's words serve as a reminder: it's not merely strength or knowledge that sets successful individuals apart but an unyielding will. When we dive into "Focus on the Big Picture," we're committing to rise above the immediate, keep our eyes on the horizon, and concentrate on what truly matters.

This focus isn't just about having a broad viewpoint; it's a conscious decision to align our actions with a larger purpose. Similar to an artist assessing their entire canvas, leaders who keep the big picture in mind ensure every detail aligns with the grander vision. They act as torchbearers, navigating their teams through the maze of daily operations toward overarching goals.

True leadership is grounded in a broader mission beyond immediate tasks. By constantly aligning with the bigger picture, leaders ensure that every decision, no matter how small, drives towards a larger purpose. This nurtures an environment where every effort paints part of a larger masterpiece of success.

Committing to the big picture is essentially a commitment to steadfast determination. It's about looking beyond short-term hurdles, remaining resilient in the face of setbacks, and fueling progress with a clear sense of purpose. Such leaders inspire a mindset of marathon-like perseverance over short sprints.

Think of it as an aviator's journey, maintaining course towards a distant destination despite any mid-flight turbulence. Leaders with a big-picture focus inspire their teams to soar above challenges, keeping their destination firmly in sight, irrespective of the obstacles.

In business, this translates to maintaining clarity and direction. By having a clear, overarching vision, these leaders foster a culture where everyone is aligned, decisions are informed, and the end goal is evident. Such a focus does more than just guide—it establishes a culture where determination is rooted in purpose.

By focusing on the big picture, you're sculpting a legacy. A legacy of purpose, enduring impact, and leadership that charts a clear course amidst the ever-changing tides of business and life.

23

H A B I T

CONTINUOUS LEARNING

*"The capacity to learn is a gift; the ability to learn is
a skill; the willingness to learn is a choice."*

—Brian Herbert

Pursuing knowledge is the life source that energizes vision, fuels innovation, and fosters growth. Brian Herbert's adage stands as a beacon, highlighting the multi-faceted nature of learning. Delving into "Continuous Learning," we uncover a dedication to ceaseless exploration, a spirit of curiosity, and the drive to ever-expand one's horizons.

Continuous learning is far more than a periodic endeavor; it's a perpetual voyage. It signifies the acknowledgment that knowledge isn't stagnant but ever-flowing. Like a diligent gardener nurturing every plant, leaders who embrace continuous learning nurture intellectual growth, sowing seeds of curiosity and reaping harvests of wisdom.

Central to this habit is recognizing leadership's ever-evolving nature. Those who ardently advocate for continuous learning understand that their growth trajectory intertwines with those they guide. By championing lifelong learning, they sow seeds in a fertile ground where everyone is motivated to evolve, question, and seek.

Embracing continuous learning is akin to setting out on an endless expedition. It's about venturing into the unknown, challenging established paradigms, and welcoming fresh perspectives. Such leaders are the torchbearers of adaptability, guiding their teams through the ever-shifting sands of progress and ensuring adaptability and resilience remain core tenets.

Imagine a dedicated scholar delving deep into volumes of knowledge, each page broadening their worldview. Leaders immersed in continuous learning emulate this scholar's spirit, kindling a desire within their teams to explore, assimilate, and apply newfound knowledge. They set the tone, exemplifying the value of intellectual pursuit and adaptability.

In the corporate world, these leaders emerge as the bedrock of innovation. By valuing and promoting relentless growth, they shape environments where learning is revered, adaptability is the norm, and progress is inevitable. Such a mindset doesn't just encourage growth; it becomes the very essence of the organization, driving both individual and shared triumphs.

When you immerse yourself in continuous learning, every piece of knowledge and lesson learned enriches your leadership ideology. It's not just about personal growth; it's about kindling that spark of curiosity in others, driving them to seek, learn, and evolve.

Let Brian Herbert's words be your compass. As you journey through the domain of continuous learning, strive to be the leader who relentlessly seeks knowledge and kindles the flames of inquisitiveness in others. In doing so, you're not just building a legacy of knowledge; you're forging a path of curiosity, adaptability, and leadership that resonates, inspires, and endures.

H A B I T

LEVERAGE NETWORKS

> *"Your network is your net worth."*
>
> —Porter Gale

I n leadership's vast web, where connections are pivotal, leveraging networks stands out as a driving force. It's like a bridge connecting various industries, pushing forward both personal and professional growth. Porter Gale's profound statement reminds us of a leadership style that goes beyond personal skills, emphasizing the transformative power of relationships.

Diving into "Leverage Networks," we see the essence of building relationships and harnessing the combined power of connections for mutual success. Networking isn't a mere hobby; it's a well-thought-out strategy. Recognizing relationships as a form of currency opens doors to myriad opportunities. Think of it like a spider crafting its web: leaders emphasizing networks create connections that embrace collaboration, knowledge exchange, and support. They become not just leaders but architects of connectivity, emphasizing the importance of a communal spirit.

True leadership isn't a solo act. It thrives on collective effort. Those who value networks understand the varied perspectives and talents they offer, acting as catalysts for innovation and progress. It promotes a collaborative environment, ensuring that the joint intelligence of a network is used for everyone's benefit.

Embracing networking is also about empowerment. It's about sharing knowledge, extending a helping hand, and celebrating others' successes. Such leaders, in essence, become pillars of reciprocity. They make it clear: when one grows, everyone benefits.

In the corporate world, networking-focused leaders leave a mark. They acknowledge the significance of relationships, fostering environments that prioritize collaboration. They champion the cause that networking isn't just a mere connection; it's a well-calibrated strategy to boost the combined potential.

As you integrate the art of networking into your leadership style, understand its impact. Every connection you establish and every bond you nurture adds to the larger framework of combined success. It not only refines your leadership but also knits a fabric of shared accomplishments.

Embracing networking embodies the ethos Porter Gale highlighted. Strive to be the leader who doesn't just connect but enables others to do the same. By emphasizing networks, you're laying down a legacy—a mark of shared victories, aspirations, and transformative leadership that stands tall in the vast arena of collaboration and growth.

25

H A B I T

ADAPT A LONG-TERM PERSPECTIVE

"In the short term, you can fool yourself and others. In the long run, the market will tell you whether you are delivering value or not."

—Jeff Bezos

The value of a long-term perspective is what turns a future leader into a successful leader. Jeff Bezos' statement captures a crucial tenet of leadership: looking beyond immediate gains for sustainable impact. When we discuss "Adapting a Long-Term Perspective," we're advocating for a vision that stretches beyond today's horizons, aiming for lasting influence.

A long-term perspective isn't just about waiting; it's about strategic planning. Like an architect designs buildings to withstand decades, leaders should frame strategies resilient enough for the future's uncertainties. This mindset elevates them from mere managers to visionaries, prioritizing sustainability over fleeting successes.

Central to this habit is the realization that leadership stretches beyond the present moment. Every decision today will echo into tomorrow. Leaders with a long-term vision are acutely aware of these ripples, focusing not just on immediate returns but on building an enduring legacy.

Taking a long-term stance requires wisdom. It means balancing immediate actions with future implications, understanding that success isn't just about immediate victories but the cumulative value delivered over time.

Think of it like gardening. A gardener doesn't just plant seeds; they nurture them, knowing well that today's effort will bear fruit in the future. Similarly, leaders should invest time and resources today, knowing the payoff might be in the distant future. It's about nurturing ideas and strategies and patiently waiting for them to mature.

In business, a long-term perspective champions resilience. Such leaders create an atmosphere where decisions aren't impulsively driven by trends but are rooted in lasting value. This kind of leadership nurtures cultures that prioritize future impact over current applause.

As you integrate a long-term view into your leadership, realize that every decision and every investment in growth craft a legacy of sustained impact. By adopting this perspective, you become more than just a leader; you become a guardian of the future.

Embrace Jeff Bezos' insight as you build this habit. Let it inspire you to lead in a way that not only meets today's challenges but also prepares for tomorrow's opportunities. With a long-term perspective, you're not just making decisions for today but shaping a legacy of lasting influence and success.

Anchoring the Habits of Strategic Thinking and Planning

As we close Chapter 5, "Strategic Thinking and Planning," we find ourselves at a juncture where dreams meet determination, where forward-thinking leaders morph into meticulous planners. This chapter was a deep dive into the nuances of leadership that interlace vision with execution and understanding with action.

From envisioning futures, setting unerring goals, and embracing the larger picture to the importance of lifelong learning and the potency of networks, each element was more than just a concept. They became intertwined, creating a cohesive blueprint for strategic leadership and connecting individual endeavors to a larger vision.

We learned about the significance of setting sights beyond the immediate and imagining futures rife with innovation and growth. In setting goals, it was evident how uniting individual aspirations with a greater mission can harmonize efforts.

Looking beyond the immediate, understanding the bigger narrative, and seeing success as a continuous journey rather than just isolated milestones became clearer. The essence of continuous learning highlighted how growth is an endless process, demanding both curiosity and commitment. Networking's emphasis revealed the infinite possibilities that emerge when we collaborate, and the long-term perspective showed us the value of sustainable strategies over fleeting success.

In closing this chapter, it's essential to remember that true leadership goes beyond just directing—it's visionary, strategic, and actionable. The principles shared here are more than just guidelines; they're the North Star for every leader aiming for impactful journeys.

In strategic thought and planning, echoes of legendary leaders remind us that our goals should always be anchored in broader horizons. Each lesson in this chapter is a piece of a larger mosaic that paints the world of leadership.

Moving forward, let's carry these lessons with us. By integrating them into our leadership ethos, we pave the way for our own growth and lay down paths for generations to follow.

So, as we step into the future, let's embrace these strategic tenets wholeheartedly. By doing so, we not only shape our destinies but also craft our futures, building a legacy that stands as a testament to true leadership—inspiring, strategic, and transformative.

CHAPTER 6

Execution and Productivity

Navigating the Path from Vision to Reality

In the vast space of leadership, hopes and dreams float like stars in the sky, lighting our way. Yet, without the two forces of execution and productivity, these dreams could stay like stars in the night sky, impossible to reach and untapped. In Chapter 6, "Execution and Productivity," we get to the heart of how to turn dreams into real results.

Execution and productivity aren't just managerial jargon. They form the pillars that uphold the journey from ideation to realization. This chapter explores tactics that meld visionary aspirations with ground-level achievements, exposing the frameworks that empower leaders to navigate through the maze of challenges, leap over hurdles, and ensure their trajectory stays true to the envisioned goal.

True leadership isn't just about charting territories; it's about leading the march across them. Just as a maestro ensures every instrument plays its part in a grand orchestral piece, leaders proficient in execution ensure that every team member's efforts contribute to the organization's overarching goals. They stand as visionary thinkers and doers, turning ideas into actionable steps.

At the heart of this chapter is a foundational belief: true leadership transcends mere strategy formation. It blossoms in strategy execution.

It's one thing to ideate, but another to actualize. Leaders who internalize this not only create an environment of planning but, more importantly, an ethos of action—a culture that values tangible outcomes over mere ideation.

Embracing execution and productivity is akin to a captain steering a ship, ensuring not just the right direction but also maintaining momentum, handling storms, and ensuring a safe arrival. It's not about just setting the destination but ensuring the journey progresses smoothly towards it.

Business leaders who prioritize these principles stand as beacons of efficiency and results. By ensuring a culture of responsibility, they inspire action and ensure results, creating a ripple effect where every team member feels the weight of their contribution.

In the landscape of execution and productivity, leadership finds its truest expression—a commitment to not just dream but to realize those dreams. Every plan made real, every milestone achieved, crafts a story of dynamic leadership—one that not only dreams but actualizes, shaping industries and setting precedents.

As we journey through this chapter, may we embrace the essence of execution, understanding that ideas, no matter how grand, only find value when realized. By imbibing the lessons of this chapter, we transition from mere dreamers to achievers, from those who aspire to those who inspire, forging paths, setting benchmarks, and redefining what it truly means to lead.

TAKE DECISIVE ACTION

"The path to success is to take massive, determined action."

—Tony Robbins

eadership is an intricate dance of thought and action, a balancing act of dreaming and doing. As we read into Habit 26, "Take Decisive Action," we see where dreams meet reality, where aspirations transform into accomplishments. Tony Robbins' words serve as a clarion call, echoing the need for determination and deliberate and unwavering momentum.

Taking decisive action transcends mere movement. It embodies the audacity to push boundaries, to challenge status quo, and to venture into uncharted territories. Just as an alchemist seeks to transmute base metals into gold, leaders embracing decisive action seek to transform challenges into opportunities, sculpting the future with intentional, bold strides.

Central to this habit is the realization that leadership isn't merely about strategic ideation; it's about the execution of those strategies. Real progress isn't born from contemplation alone but from the marriage of vision and veracity, of dreams and dauntless endeavors. Leaders rooted in this principle foster an environment where action is not just encouraged but expected. They instill a sense of urgency, propelling their teams toward proactive pursuits rather than reactive responses.

Embracing decisive action is like charting a voyage. It demands not just setting the course but also bravely navigating through storms, steering the ship with unwavering focus, and ensuring it remains on its desired trajectory. Leaders who champion this habit act as both the compass and the captain, guiding their teams through complexities and driving forward with unwavering commitment.

In the corporate sphere, decisive action serves as the catalyst for innovation, growth, and transformative results. Such leaders, by promoting proactive problem-solving, calculated risk-taking, and a relentless pursuit of excellence, create a vibrant atmosphere where stagnation is the enemy and innovation the ally. Their ethos resonates, creating waves of proactive energy that ripple throughout the organization, igniting fires of enthusiasm and commitment.

As you immerse yourself in the spirit of this habit, remember that every action, every leap, and every step forward shapes the narrative of your leadership journey. Each challenge faced and hurdle surmounted testifies to a leadership style unyielding in its pursuit of greatness. By taking decisive action, you stand as a beacon of vision and a testament to the power of tenacity and transformative change.

As you embody the ethos of taking decisive action, let Robbins' wisdom be the wind beneath your wings, driving you towards audacious heights. Commit to being a leader who does more than just envision the future; be the one who shapes it. By championing decisive action, you etch a legacy of impactful leadership—a legacy that inspires, influences, and invokes change, leaving a lasting imprint on the annals of achievement.

H A B I T

STREAMLINE PROCESSES

"Efficiency is doing things right. Effectiveness is doing the right things."

—Peter Drucker

eadership is a dynamic blend of vision and execution, where the canvas of ideas meets the brushstrokes of implementation. Within this complex artwork lies the habit of streamlining our processes, a guiding principle that ensures each brushstroke contributes meaningfully to the final masterpiece. Drucker's aphorism is a beacon, highlighting the need for harmonizing efficiency with purposeful direction.

Streamlining processes goes beyond mere simplification. It's the alchemy of transforming cluttered operations into an orchestra of synchronized activities. Like an orchestrator who seamlessly integrates various instruments into a singular, impactful melody, leaders adept at streamlining processes harmonize the different operational elements to achieve optimal outcomes.

The heart of this habit underscores the belief that leadership isn't just about reaching the finish line but also about optimizing the journey. Streamlined processes ensure that every step taken is purposeful, every resource utilized is maximized, and every action embarked upon aligns with overarching goals. By fostering this culture, leaders champion a mindset where teams don't just work harder but work smarter.

The path to streamlining processes is paved with introspection and innovation. It necessitates a willingness to dissect existing workflows, discern inefficiencies, and design pathways that align operational endeavors with strategic intentions. Leaders who immerse themselves in this journey stand as pioneers, setting benchmarks of excellence and propelling their teams toward best practices that amalgamate efficiency and effectiveness.

Drawing upon a potter molding clay analogy, leaders delve into process refinement mold operations with precision, ensuring that each curve, contour, and nuance contributes to the desired outcome. Their interventions act as the artisan's hands, shaping, refining, and perfecting, ensuring the end product is a testament to the beauty of streamlined endeavor.

In the corporate echelons, streamlining is more than a methodology; it's a mindset. Leaders anchoring on this habit drive a narrative of operational excellence, pushing boundaries, challenging conventions, and instilling an ethos where efficiency marries effectiveness. This narrative permeates the organization's fabric, creating a process where every task, no matter how mundane, is seen through the optimization lens.

As you internalize the essence of this habit, let each refinement, each enhancement, and each innovation stand as a chapter in your leadership odyssey. Understand that streamlining isn't about cutting corners but enhancing the journey, ensuring every stride is meaningful and impactful. By championing streamlined processes, you emerge as a leader of action and an optimized action orchestrator.

HABIT

28

MANAGE ENERGY, NOT JUST TIME

"Don't count the days, make the days count."

—Muhammad Ali

The habit of managing energy, rather than just time, acts as a guiding light for leaders, helping them tap into their inner vitality and purpose. Managing energy goes beyond simply organizing one's schedule. It is the deep art of accessing one's inner wellspring of passion, purpose, and mindfulness. Leaders who are skilled at managing their energy approach their days with intentionality. They make sure that every task, no matter how mundane, is filled with meaning.

At the core of this habit is recognizing that leadership is not a sprint against the clock but a marathon of purpose and passion. Such leaders understand that the true measure of impactful leadership isn't the number of hours logged, but the energy and purpose poured into those hours. This philosophy births a culture where value is placed on meaningful engagement over mere presence.

The journey to managing energy over time is one of introspection, rejuvenation, and alignment. Leaders must delve deep, understand their core drivers, and align their tasks with their innate strengths and passions.

Leaders on this journey are guardians of well-being, emphasizing the importance of recharging, refocusing, and realigning for sustained impact.

Imagine an artist meticulously crafting a piece, pouring their soul into every intricate detail. Leaders who adeptly manage energy become similar artists, inspiring teams to pour their essence into their roles, ensuring each task undertaken becomes a masterpiece of purpose. Their leadership offers the blueprint for others to craft their roles with intentionality and vigor.

Within the organizational structure, these leaders stand as champions of holistic well-being. By endorsing practices that align with individual energies, promoting breaks, and emphasizing the importance of passion-driven roles, they foster an environment where well-being and productivity coalesce. Their leadership radiates, promoting a culture where every task undertaken is a mirror reflecting purposeful energy.

As you internalize this habit, may each moment you spend and each task you undertake become a testament to your commitment to managing energy, not just time. Understand that it's about filling the hours and fueling them with purpose. In managing energy, you emerge as a leader of tasks and a beacon of purposeful passion.

Take Ali's wisdom and let it guide your energy management. Craft a legacy where every second is an echo of purposeful energy. By managing energy over mere time, you shape your narrative and inspire others to craft a story bursting with vitality, purpose, and profound impact.

H A B I T

FOCUS ON HIGH-IMPACT ACTIVITIES

"You can do anything, but not everything."

—David Allen

ocusing on high-impact activities is like selecting the right brushstrokes for an artist's masterpiece. David Allen's profound words underscore the value of discernment—prioritizing tasks that make a difference over those that simply keep us busy. Embracing "Focus on High-Impact Activities" is a commitment to value substance over volume, ensuring our energy leads to meaningful results.

This isn't just about efficient time management; it's about the purposeful allocation of effort. Think of a composer weaving together melodies to form a grand symphony. Similarly, leaders emphasizing high-impact activities harmonize their goals, strategies, and actions to create a coherent narrative of success. They become architects of intention, ensuring clarity in purpose and execution.

Leadership is less about the number of tasks tackled and more about the quality of outcomes achieved. By prioritizing high-impact activities, leaders emphasize strategic focus over mere busyness. This approach fosters a culture where actions aren't just about ticking boxes but about creating real, tangible change.

Navigating this path requires a clear vision—to overlook distractions, concentrate on what truly matters, and ensure resources are invested wisely. Such leaders guide their teams with clarity of purpose, ensuring that everyone's efforts align with overarching goals. The result is a culture where productivity is paired with purpose.

Imagine an artist whose strokes are deliberate and filled with intention. Such is the approach of leaders who focus on high-impact activities. They inspire teams to work with precision, crafting outcomes that truly make a difference. Their leadership becomes an art form, combining strategy and execution, leading to purposeful achievements.

In business, this focus translates into a framework of efficiency. Leaders who champion high-impact activities foster an environment where every decision is driven by its potential to bring about change. Their influence encourages teams to dedicate their energy to what truly drives progress.

Embracing this habit is about shaping your leadership legacy. Every decision and every prioritized task becomes a testament to a leadership style that values impact over activity. It's about being intentional, strategic, and transformative.

As you delve into focusing on high-impact activities, let David Allen's wisdom be your compass. Strive to be a leader who doesn't just prioritize but inspires others to do the same. In doing so, you craft a legacy of impactful achievements and purposeful leadership—a testament to the art of leading with intention.

HABIT

DEVELOP A BIAS FOR ACTION

"The best way to predict the future is to create it."

—Peter Drucker

eadership isn't just about visions; it's about bold actions. Within the "Develop a Bias for Action" concept, leaders are not just bystanders watching the future unfold; they're sculptors, actively chiseling their desired future.

Having a bias for action isn't about mere movement; it's a proactive mindset. It means seeing potential, grasping opportunities, and transforming ideas into tangible results. Think of a sculptor tirelessly molding clay into a masterpiece. Similarly, effective leaders transform aspirations into achievements by acting decisively, embracing challenges, and being adaptable.

True leadership isn't a spectator's game. It's participatory, with a dynamic interplay between intent and execution. Leaders with a genuine bias for action understand that progress isn't born from idle contemplation but from the courage to embrace uncertainty and challenge the status quo.

This bias is a commitment to action. Leaders who adopt it guide their teams with a pioneering spirit, advocating for innovation and experimentation. They promote an environment where every team member feels inspired to act, take risks, and make impactful contributions.

Imagine an inventor relentlessly pursuing new ideas, breaking barriers, and turning imagination into reality. Leaders with a bias for action mirror this spirit, motivating their teams to see challenges as opportunities, to push boundaries, and to become architects of change.

In business, these leaders promote a culture where initiative is rewarded and risks are seen as pathways to innovation. Their influence cultivates environments where progress is intentional and every individual feels they have a stake in the company's success.

Embracing this habit means remembering that every action and every decision contributes to the legacy of dynamic leadership and transformative progress. By developing this bias, you don't just dream; you act, becoming a beacon of transformative leadership.

As you venture deeper into the ethos of action, let Peter Drucker's wisdom guide you. Strive to be the leader who dreams and galvanizes others into action. By encouraging this bias for action, you create a legacy that is characterized by deliberate change, proactive growth, and persuasive leadership—painting a future that you not only predict but also actively create.

Anchoring the Habits of Execution and Productivity

As the final notes of Chapter 6, "Execution and Productivity," we stand on the cusp of enlightenment—an inflection point where visions metamorphose into victories, dreams morph into deliverables, and the beacon of purposeful leadership shines brightest. This chapter was not merely an exposition but a masterclass that underscored the alchemy of turning potential into performance through an unwavering focus on the pillars of proactive decision-making, streamlined execution, and purpose-driven momentum.

Navigating the vast terrains of this chapter, we witnessed the interplay of crucial leadership imperatives: the courage of decisiveness, the beauty of lean processes, the art of energy optimization, the sagacity of emphasizing high-impact actions, and the vitality of a relentless bias towards action. These weren't mere standalone tenets; they formed the intricate fabric of what it means to execute with vision and yield results with resonance.

From seeing leaders transcend the paralysis of over-analysis to action to appreciating the finesse with which complexities were distilled into fluid processes, this chapter was a tribute to leadership in its most authentic and impactful form.

The narratives around energy management underscored that it's not the number of hours that matter, but the substance packed within them. The discourse on high-impact activities was a clarion call to eschew the noise and zone in on what truly shifts the needle. And as for cultivating a bias for action? It's a clarion call for leaders to be not just dreamers but doers, architects of the future, and agents of change.

As we turn the page on this chapter, it's imperative to internalize and champion its core essence. Remember, true leadership doesn't manifest in mere motion but in meaningful milestones. The insights from this chapter are not just waypoints but the very compass that will guide our leadership odysseys.

In the grand concert of execution and productivity, every leader is both a maestro and a musician—setting the tone, pace, and rhythm while synchronizing with the larger ensemble. The melodies produced, resonating with purpose and passion, not only uplift organizations but redefine industries, catalyze innovation, and sculpt legacies.

As we venture ahead, let's not merely adhere to the tenets of this chapter but embody them. By intertwining these principles with our leadership DNA, we champion a legacy of unparalleled excellence—a legacy that doesn't just chronicle our individual journeys but inspires generations, catalyzing a movement of purpose, passion, and unparalleled productivity.

CHAPTER 7

Influence and Negotiation

INTRODUCTION
The Art of Persuasion and the Dance of Diplomacy

Collaboration is a key part of leadership, and the subtle art of persuasion is the compass that guides change. In this chapter, "Influence and Negotiation," we look at how persuasion and diplomacy work together to create the blueprint for strong leadership. This chapter takes us into the heart of human interaction, where the skills to inspire, persuade, and negotiate become the pillars of making alliances, making decisions, and making progress.

This chapter delves into the dance between the innate art of building connections and the strategy of aligning divergent views. It's about building rapport, sharing visions, and forming a consensus, all while navigating a mosaic of perspectives, unifying goals, and bridging differences. As we explore charisma, empathy, persuasion, and negotiation, we uncover leadership's core principles that individuals, teams, and entire organizations can use.

True leadership transcends mere authority. It's about lighting the way, shaping outcomes, and resonating through influence. Imagine a maestro directing an orchestra: such is the leader who shines in this domain, seamlessly blending varying tones, resolving conflicts, and ensuring every voice elevates the collective performance.

Central to this chapter is the realization that leadership flourishes not in isolation but in a symphony of relationships and interactions. Here, the tenets of influence and negotiation come into play, offering leaders a compass to traverse the complex landscape of human dynamics, igniting action, syncing visions, and crafting alliances that herald collective advancement.

But influence and negotiation are more than just skills. They have a language of their own, speaking through gestures, expressions, and deep-rooted empathy. Like an artist expressing emotions with every brushstroke, leaders adept in these areas deftly convey intentions, fostering shared understanding. They stand out as beacons of clarity, promoting leadership that echoes with both precision and authenticity.

In the business world, these leaders are peacekeepers. They forge connections, mediate disputes, and nurture a culture of proactive engagement. With their influential touch, they rally teams behind a shared mission, and with their negotiation prowess, they align varied interests, ensuring collective benefits.

As we navigate "Influence and Negotiation," let's champion the ethos of collaboration and impactful communication. The insights from this chapter refine our leadership repertoire and position us as agents of change, ambassadors of influence, and strategic harmonizers. In understanding and mastering influence and negotiation, we're setting the stage for a leadership style that not only dreams big but also adeptly maneuvers human dynamics to turn those dreams into reality.

H A B I T

DEVELOP PERSUASIVE COMMUNICATION

"If you just communicate, you can get by. But if you communicate skillfully, you can work miracles."

—Jim Rohn

Communication is the foundation of leadership. But persuasive communication? That's the essence of truly impactful leadership. Echoing Jim Rohn's sentiment, it's the difference between simply getting by and making significant, transformative strides. As we delve into "developing persuasive communication," we're exploring not just the art of talking but the mastery of truly connecting and being influential in our dialogues.

This is no superficial skill. Persuasive communication is an art, with each word carefully chosen, each gesture delicately employed, and each message meticulously crafted. Like a poet capturing emotions, leaders with this skill can truly resonate, inspire, and guide. They don't just convey information; they ignite understanding and drive purposeful action.

True leadership isn't about merely giving orders. It's about fostering alignment, shared visions, and mutual aspirations. Persuasive communicators understand this intuitively. Their words do more than deliver messages—they shape perceptions, build genuine rapport and influence decisions. In the hands of such leaders, every conversation is an opportunity, an avenue to inspire progress and foster engagement.

Imagine a master composer, with each note of their symphony meticulously selected to convey an emotion or tell a story. Leaders skilled in persuasive communication are akin to these composers, except their symphony is one of words, expressions, and shared visions. They recognize the deep power of communication as a skill and a force that can transform.

Business leaders who master this skill become influencers, fostering an environment where ideas aren't just thrown around—they're embraced, understood, and acted upon. Their influence permeates, creating workplaces where effective communication is the gold standard and shaping a culture of genuine collaboration.

So, as you commit to mastering persuasive communication, remember every word you speak and every dialogue you engage in is a brushstroke in the portrait of your leadership legacy. Harness this art, and not only will you connect, inspire, and lead more effectively, but you'll leave a lasting impact, truly embodying the wisdom of Jim Rohn. Through refined communication, leaders convey messages and inspire, influence, and truly lead, leaving an indelible mark on the path of influential dialogue.

HABIT

BUILD STRONG RELATIONSHIPS: THE KEYSTONE OF COLLABORATIVE LEADERSHIP

"You can't do today's job with yesterday's methods and be in business tomorrow."

—George W. Bush

The most powerful leaders stand on a foundation built on trust, collaboration, and genuine connections. The sentiment of former President George W. Bush points towards adaptability and evolving, and at the core of this is nurturing relationships.

Building relationships isn't about schmoozing at networking events. It's about truly engaging, understanding, and valuing each interaction, recognizing that these connections often form the bedrock of sustained success. Like a builder placing each brick with precision and care, leaders emphasizing relationship-building foster an environment of trust, shared purpose, and mutual growth.

True leadership is not a solo mission. It's about bringing everyone along, valuing their contributions, and understanding the power of combined effort. Leaders who place relationships at the center of their strategy understand that their connections amplify their strength. Each engagement becomes a chance to connect and deepen ties, ensuring a shared path toward success.

Relationship-building is about recognizing the strengths in others, valuing their perspectives, and creating an inclusive environment where collaboration is more than a buzzword—it's the norm. Such leaders, by their actions, emphasize that an organization's true strength lies in its collective effort, diversity, and shared sense of purpose.

Imagine a gardener who knows that while each plant is unique, when they come together, they create a garden of unparalleled beauty. Similarly, leaders who focus on relationship-building understand the unique value of each team member and know that when harmoniously combined, they create an entity much greater than the sum of its parts.

In business, fostering strong relationships means being attuned to change, ready to adapt, and always ensuring an environment where trust and collaboration thrive. Such leaders don't just create teams; they build interconnected units where every individual feels valued and heard.

So, as you walk the path of nurturing relationships, remember: every interaction, every shared moment, is a step towards creating an enduring legacy. Each genuine connection and mutual respect defines the trajectory of your leadership journey. By emphasizing relationships, you not only foster trust but also create a vibrant, connected community ready to face any challenge.

H A B I T

SEEK WIN-WIN SOLUTIONS

> *"You can't make decisions based on fear and the possibility of what might happen."*
>
> —Michelle Obama

At its core, leadership is the dance of unity in the face of diversity—an elegant choreography of merging contrasting aspirations into a harmonious rhythm. Guided by Michelle Obama's wisdom, leaders transcending traditional adversarial boundaries acknowledge that the magic habit of seeking win-win solutions lies in the interplay of shared objectives. This isn't merely about compromise; it's an evolved approach to fostering mutual growth and prosperity.

The pursuit of win-win solutions transcends mere tactics; it reflects a philosophy. A true leader understands that the essence of leadership isn't about overpowering but about harmonizing. Like a conductor leading an orchestra, blending individual notes into a symphonic masterpiece, leaders who embrace win-win solutions craft strategies that harmonize diverse interests, creating a melody of shared success.

In the heart of this approach lies the belief that leadership isn't a battle to be won but a journey to be shared. Such leaders are driven not by conquest but by collaboration. In their approach, every challenge presents an opportunity to create shared value, ensuring each stakeholder feels seen, heard, and valued.

Adopting a win-win mentality means rising above the primal instincts of competition and viewing challenges through collaboration. Such leaders are not just problem solvers but bridge builders, uniting diverse aspirations and converting potential conflicts into opportunities for collective growth.

Imagine a welder meticulously blending different metals into a strong and beautiful alloy. Leaders who champion win-win solutions merge diverse perspectives, ensuring that the resultant blend is stronger, more resilient, and reflective of collective aspirations.

In the corporate world, where challenges are as constant as change, leaders committed to win-win outcomes foster an environment where every negotiation is seen as a canvas of possibilities. Their approach creates a culture where the goal isn't to win but to rise together, ensuring that the journey forward is marked by shared milestones and collective triumphs.

As you internalize the win-win mindset, recognize the transformative power of this approach. Every negotiation and every dialogue you partake in is an opportunity to weave a narrative of shared success. You craft a legacy of unity, mutual respect, and collective prosperity by championing mutual benefit.

Guided by Michelle Obama's profound insights, may the ethos of collaboration illuminate your leadership journey. By embracing win-win solutions, you lead with vision and heart, crafting a legacy that is both impactful and enduring.

34

H A B I T

PRACTICE ASSERTIVENESS

"I've learned that people will forget what you said, people will forget what you did, but people will never forget how you made them feel."

—Maya Angelou

Assertiveness is a strong and clear pillar of leadership, where words shape futures and interactions create legacies. Leadership is more than just telling people what to do. It goes beyond that and into real connection, where the essence of the message leaves marks much deeper than words could.

Assertiveness, often misinterpreted as aggression, is, in reality, a manifestation of authentic self-expression. True leadership doesn't overshadow; it illuminates, allowing for an environment where perspectives shine with mutual respect. Like an artist meticulously sketching on a canvas, leaders who value assertiveness craft interactions that balance confidence with empathy, ensuring messages resonate while preserving the harmony of relationships.

Central to this habit is the realization that leadership isn't a monologue but a dialogue. Leaders who champion assertiveness understand that progress isn't born out of silent agreement but from the vibrant interplay of diverse voices. By adopting an assertive stance, they build spaces where every voice, regardless of its volume, is acknowledged and where every idea, no matter its origin, finds a receptive audience.

Embracing assertiveness is an ode to empowerment. It signifies a leader's commitment to value their own insights while opening doors to others' viewpoints. Leaders anchored in this principle serve as beacons of self-confidence, guiding teams towards realizing their inherent worth, championing transparent communication, and fostering a milieu where feedback becomes a chance for collective growth.

Leaders who emphasize assertiveness set the stage for progressive discourse and innovation in organizational spheres. They champion environments where confidence is met with appreciation and where candid discussions pave the way for breakthrough solutions. Such cultures don't see assertiveness as confrontational; instead, they celebrate it as a catalyst for innovation and progress.

With every assertive stance you adopt and every environment you cultivate where voices are celebrated, you're sculpting a legacy of empathetic leadership and influential dialogues. With each endeavor, you're leading with conviction and inspiring a wave of confident communicators.

As you mold this habit, may you be inspired by the clarity of your words and the profound impact of your authentic expression. In practicing assertiveness, you etch a legacy of empowered interactions, authentic engagements, and influential leadership, shaping your narrative and inspiring countless others in the language of impactful communication.

H A B I T

UNDERSTAND THE POWER OF PERSUASION

> *"Influence is the key to any leadership."*
>
> —John C. Maxwell

U nderstanding the power of persuasion is one of the most critical aspects of leadership. John C. Maxwell's ideas led to a profound realization: leadership is more than just a title; it involves shaping minds, inspiring hearts, and guiding actions. When we enter the world of "Harnessing Persuasion," we are asked to go on a journey to master the subtle art of persuasion, craft persuasive stories, and lead with charisma that inspires and motivates people to work together.

Persuasion, not manipulation, is a blend of genuine connection and visionary guidance. Leadership isn't about issuing mandates; it's about painting a vivid picture, a shared dream, and inspiring others to journey to-wards it. The soul of this habit hinges on a profound realization: leadership is about unity. Leaders who truly understand the power of persuasion are adept at speaking the language of the heart, bridging individual aspirations to a collective vision, and inspiring teams to traverse the path of challenges in pursuit of a shared destiny. By adopting this philosophy, they foster an environment where every dialogue is an opportunity to inspire and every message is a beacon, guiding towards shared goals.

Embracing the nuances of persuasion is like navigating the vast expanse of human emotions and aspirations. Leaders attuned to this art emerge as beacons of inspiration, unraveling the threads of potential in individuals and teams and fostering dialogues that transcend mere communication and transform visions into tangible realities. Their influence becomes the undercurrent that fuels creativity, enkindles passion, and propels organizations into arenas of groundbreaking achievements.

Imagine a lighthouse standing tall amidst stormy seas, guiding ships safely to the harbor. Leaders skilled in persuasion mirror this image, offering direction amidst uncertainties, instilling confidence, and guiding teams toward the shores of collective success. Their leadership isn't about domineering but about illuminating the path and understanding that persuasion is more about inspiration than imposition.

Within organizational ecosystems, leaders rooted in persuasion emerge as catalysts for synergy and alignment. By valuing and mastering influential leadership, they architect environments where individuals are more than just contributors; they become co-authors of a shared success story. Such leadership imprints itself deep within the organization's DNA, championing a culture where persuasion is celebrated as a vehicle of unity, inspiration, and groundbreaking progress.

As you tread the path of harnessing persuasion, acknowledge the vast canvas of your influence. Every story you share, every vision you portray, and every connection you foster will craft your legacy of transformational leadership and profound influence. Each endeavor, every gesture, and every word is a testament to your commitment to lead not just from a position of authority but from a place of genuine connection and inspiration.

Anchoring the Habits of Influence and Negotiation

In the multifaceted world of leadership, communication is the backbone that fosters unity while influence drives progress forward. "Influence and Negotiation" concludes, having delved into the art of persuasion, the rhythm of negotiations, and the shared dance of collaboration. Reflecting upon this journey, we stand at the heart of effective leadership, where inspiring others, building consensus, and fostering collaboration meld to form a meaningful legacy.

Through "Influence and Negotiation," we've unraveled the subtle intricacies of leadership that go beyond mere titles. We've explored the art of persuasive dialogues that breathe life into words and assertive conversations that allow voices to shine with authenticity. Moreover, we've discovered cooperative negotiation, a space where successes are mutual and sculpted with understanding, respect, and the delicate balance of give and take.

At this chapter's core, we recognize that leadership is not just about guiding but also about connecting. It's about understanding that influence isn't built on dominance but on the ability to touch hearts and unify teams toward shared visions. Negotiation isn't a game of winners or losers but a dance of collaboration, finding harmony in different viewpoints, and orchestrating a shared success story.

As this chapter closes, let's remember that true leadership lies in the relationships we build, the change we inspire, and the potential we recognize and nurture. The principles of influence and negotiation provide us with the tools to build bridges of understanding, motivate change, and navigate the intricate dynamics of human relationships with empathy and insight.

Influence and negotiation, beyond techniques, are the pillars of impactful leadership. They're languages that echo our shared humanity, guiding us toward common goals and reflecting our ability to lead collectively. By mastering these skills, we become more than just leaders; we become facilitators of unity and progress.

Moving forward, let's cherish the ever-evolving symphony of leadership enriched by every conversation, agreement, and connection we foster. With the lessons from influence and negotiation, we're not just marking our journey but shaping a legacy that champions collaboration, understanding, and positive change.

CHAPTER 8

Resilience and Overcoming Challenges

INTRODUCTION
Leadership in the Face of Adversity

With its twists and turns, valleys, and peaks, leadership shines brightest when navigating the chapter "Resilience and Overcoming Challenges." This chapter unveils the art of braving life's storms, mastering uncertainty, and emerging resilient after facing adversity. Within these challenges, leaders aren't merely tested; they're molded. The fires of adversity shape their character, fortifying their determination and honing their adaptability, thus preparing them to lead with an unyielding spirit and clarity of purpose.

Resilience and tackling challenges aren't just themes; they are the anvil on which true leadership is sculpted. In the same vein as a blacksmith perfecting steel, leaders bolster their tenacity, adaptability, and emotional strength, becoming a bastion of fortitude amidst life's unpredictable winds. Such leaders symbolize endurance, epitomizing a spirit that doesn't just withstand adversity but grows stronger, lighting the way for others.

How a leader responds to challenges, not whether there are any, is central to this chapter. Resilient leaders see setbacks not as defeats but growth opportunities, obstacles as innovation catalysts, and difficulties as avenues for positive transformation. By internalizing this philosophy, they foster an environment of audacity, meeting every setback flexibly and ensuring that challenges only reinforce their dedication to thrive.

Embarking on the journey of resilience and challenge-overcoming means making a pact to rise beyond the circumstances and to steer through uncharted challenges with grace and ingenuity. Such leaders become torchbearers, inspiring teams to perceive adversities not as hindrances but as gateways to excellence. Their perseverance serves as a guiding light, reminding everyone that the journey to success may be punctuated with ups and downs, but the destination remains the same.

Envision a climber relentlessly pursuing a mountain's summit despite overwhelming odds. Leaders championing resilience mirror this climber, motivating their teams to overcome unique challenges and tread distinctive paths. Their journey, though filled with obstacles, serves as a testament to their undying spirit and an inspiration to others.

In the corporate world, resilient leaders are pillars of adaptability and innovation. Promoting a culture of resourcefulness, they shape spaces where individuals are geared to embrace change, understand uncertainty, and confront challenges fearlessly. Such a leadership ethos reverberates through the organization, instilling a resilience-centric mindset where challenges metamorphose into chances.

As we traverse the path of resilience, we will harness an unwavering spirit. Drawing inspiration from those who've battled adversities and emerged triumphant, we should remember that the essence of leadership lies not in avoiding challenges but in turning them into opportunities for growth.

HABIT 36

EMBRACE FAILURE

"Success is stumbling from failure to failure with no loss of enthusiasm."

—Winston Churchill

Every leader's journey is interspersed with moments of victory and lessons from setbacks. Winston Churchill's words remind us of an enduring principle: the true essence of leadership isn't avoiding failures but harnessing them toward success. In the chapter "Embrace Failure," we delve into understanding failure not as a sign of weakness but as an avenue for growth and innovation.

Embracing failure isn't about celebrating mistakes but about recognizing the courage it takes to learn from them. Think of an artist. Not every stroke they make creates a masterpiece, but each attempt contributes to their evolution. Similarly, effective leaders understand the value of venturing into the unknown, challenging the familiar, and learning from the outcomes, good or bad. Doing so fosters an environment where risks are seen as gateways to innovation.

Central to this habit is the idea that every setback paves the way for a comeback. Effective leaders don't shy away from failure. Instead, they analyze, learn from, and use them as fuel for future endeavors. It's about nurturing a mindset where curiosity overrules fear and where setbacks are not dead ends but detours guiding us toward a better path.

Think of a trailblazing explorer setting foot on unknown terrain, driven by sheer curiosity and determination. Sometimes they find treasure, sometimes, they hit a dead end, but every step is progress. Similarly, leaders who embrace failure inspire their teams to push boundaries, question norms, and remain undeterred by occasional missteps. Their journey, like that of explorers, teaches that the real treasure lies in the journey itself and the lessons derived from it.

In the business world, this perspective is game-changing. Leaders who welcome failures as learning experiences foster a culture of innovation where risks are encouraged and learning is continuous. Such environments don't see failure as a setback but as feedback, vital for growth.

So, as we internalize the habit of embracing failure, let's remember: it's not about never failing but about never giving up. Let's be inspired by those who've transformed their failures into springboards for success. By doing so, we're not just navigating our path but also charting a course for future leaders, teaching them that in leadership and innovation, it's not the fall but the rise that defines us.

37

H A B I T

STAY COMMITTED TO PURPOSE

"The best way to find yourself is to lose yourself in the service of others."

—Mahatma Gandhi

L eadership is a mosaic of vision, action, and purpose. Mahatma Gandhi's wisdom reminds us that true self-discovery often stems from dedicating oneself to others. In committing to our purpose, we harness the heart of leadership that seeks not personal acclaim but the transformative impact of serving a purpose greater than oneself.

Purpose is more than just a word—it's a calling. It's not about losing oneself but about finding fulfillment in avenues larger than individual ambitions. Think of an architect: they don't just build structures; they craft legacies for communities. Similarly, leaders devoted to purpose not only guide but inspire, ensuring their impact resonates beyond boardrooms and touches lives and communities.

True leadership isn't a solitary journey of personal accolades but a collective expedition of making positive differences. Leaders dedicated to purpose understand that their greatest achievements aren't measured in profits or promotions but in the positive ripples they create in the world.

Such leadership fosters environments where compassion becomes the compass, guiding decisions and actions towards the greater good.

A gardener's joy isn't merely in the act of planting but in witnessing the blossoms that bring joy to others. Purpose-driven leaders are like these gardeners, cultivating environments that foster growth, unity, and positive change. Their leadership isn't just about strategy but about nurturing spaces where every individual feels valued and can thrive.

In business, purpose isn't just a tagline. Leaders who truly embed purpose in their ethos create ripple effects, building cultures where the spirit of service transcends job descriptions. Their influence fosters organizations where purpose is the heartbeat, guiding actions, decisions, and innovations.

So, as we get into the habit of staying committed to purpose, let's not merely focus on our journey but on the paths we illuminate for others. Inspired by those who've made service their legacy, let's remember that true leadership isn't about standing in the spotlight but ensuring it shines on those we serve. By embracing purpose, we create footprints of change, impact, and heartfelt service.

HABIT

MANAGE STRESS AND PRESSURE

> *"The greatest weapon against stress is our ability to choose one thought over another."*
>
> —William James

L eadership often feels like a dance with unpredictability. In this dynamic, high-pressure environment, William James' wisdom reminds us that our thoughts are both our anchor and our compass. In "Manage Stress and Pressure," we unravel the art of maintaining clarity amidst chaos, choosing mindful resilience over-reactive despair.

Stress isn't a sign of incompetence but a reality of leadership. Rather than an invitation to retreat, it's an opportunity to rise. Imagine a seasoned sailor navigating turbulent waves; their prowess isn't in avoiding storms but in steering with calm assurance. Similarly, adept leaders don't sidestep stress; they harness its energy, channeling it into purposeful direction and action.

Central to this habit is a commitment to self-awareness and well-being. Leadership isn't a sprint but a marathon, requiring not just mental acuity but emotional and physical stamina. Those at the helm of leadership, armed with the tools of self-care and mindfulness, create an oasis of calm even amidst whirlwinds, grounding their teams and decisions in balanced reflection.

Leadership resilience isn't about donning an armor of invulnerability but cultivating a heart of adaptability. Those who master stress management are like seasoned athletes, viewing challenges as avenues to hone their craft, not threats to their capability. They champion a culture where stress isn't shunned but skillfully channeled into innovation and insight.

Picture a potter molding clay. With gentle yet firm touches, the raw material is transformed into art. Leaders adept at managing stress likewise mold circumstances, turning pressures into pathways for growth. Their example encourages teams to not just endure challenges but to embrace them as catalysts for creativity and cohesion.

In the corporate arena, leaders who emphasize mindfulness and emotional agility lay the foundation for holistic success. By advocating practices that transform stress from a foe to an ally, they sculpt organizations where well-being isn't a luxury but a linchpin of sustained performance.

In our journey through the corridors of leadership, let's arm ourselves with the shield of emotional agility and the compass of mindfulness. Drawing from the resilience of those who've steered through storms with elegance, we're reminded that true leadership doesn't lie in evading stress but in elegantly navigating it. Through mindful resilience, we not only elevate our leadership narrative but also etch a legacy of balance, brilliance, and boundless potential.

HABIT

LEARN FROM MISTAKES

"The only real mistake is the one from which we learn nothing."

—Henry Ford

Leadership is created from experiences, mistakes, and lessons learned. As Henry Ford wisely notes, the true mistake is not in making errors, but in failing to grasp the lessons they hold. As we begin to learn from our mistakes, we recognize the skill of embracing imperfections not as hindrances, but as chances for transformation, refinement, and growth.

To err is human, but to learn from and grow from those errors is the hallmark of effective leadership. Rather than being cloaked in infallibility, true leaders embody the vulnerability and humility to admit, reflect upon, and benefit from their blunders.

Embedded in this habit is the realization that leadership is a continuum of growth, a journey where every stumble is an invitation for introspection. Leaders who imbibe this philosophy understand that perfection is not the goal; perpetual evolution is. This iterative process, much like a potter shaping clay, involves molding and remolding until the desired form emerges.

Leadership steeped in reflective evolution acknowledges the power of feedback loops. It involves a keenness to ask, "What did we learn? How can we do better? It's a practice of viewing challenges not as dead-ends but as detours leading to innovative solutions. Those who master this art nurture environments where teams are unafraid to take calculated risks, knowing that they'll either succeed or learn a lesson.

Think of a scientist in a laboratory where every experiment, regardless of its outcome, yields valuable data. Leaders who adeptly learn from mistakes are analogous to these scientists, fostering a culture where failures are not futile but are fertile grounds for growth.

Business leaders advocating this growth mindset position themselves at the forefront of innovation. By celebrating the spirit of inquiry and encouraging the courage to falter, they catalyze environments of dynamic adaptability. Here, every misstep amplifies the collective intelligence as teams rally to dissect, understand, and advance from them.

As we champion the habit of learning from mistakes, let's remember that the mightiest oak trees grow from small acorns and their share of storms. Drawing wisdom from those who have pivoted from pitfalls, we discern that leadership's essence isn't in evading errors but in sculpting success stories from them. By learning from mistakes, we inscribe a narrative of relentless self-improvement, adaptive resilience, and inspired leadership—a narrative that enriches our journey and imprints lasting imprints on the annals of visionary leadership.

HABIT

FOSTER A POSITIVE MINDSET

"Optimism is the faith that leads to achievement. Nothing can be done without hope and confidence."

—Helen Keller

Fostering a positive mindset is the road we take to inspiration, resilience, and a firm belief in the power of possibility. Helen Keller's words are timeless truths that capture the essence of leadership that goes beyond problems to embrace the transformative power of optimism. This power gives leaders the ability to give people hope, spread positivity, and lead people and teams to success and achievement. When we foster positive mindsets, we make a promise to cultivate optimism, grow a "can-do" attitude, and use the positive leadership that pushes us toward excellence.

We must understand that fostering a positive mindset doesn't mean overlooking challenges or being oblivious to potential pitfalls. It means viewing these challenges as opportunities waiting to be harnessed. Much like the sunflower that turns toward the sun, leaders with a positive mindset turn toward solutions, innovation, and progress, ensuring their teams do the same.

A positive mindset is more than just a sunny disposition. It's a strategy, a guiding principle, and a tool in the leader's arsenal. When leaders imbibe this philosophy, they're not just exuding optimism but infusing their teams with a sense of purpose, belief, and resilience. Every hurdle, every setback, and every challenge an becomes an opportunity invitation for innovation.

Navigating leadership with a positive mindset is akin to a sailor steering their ship with a compass always pointing to their true north. These leaders don't just stay on course; they inspire their crew to believe in the journey, assuring them that the destination is worth every storm they weather together.

Picture a flame. Even the smallest candle can light up a dark room. Leaders who foster a positive mindset are those flames. They illuminate the path for themselves and their entire organization, ensuring that even in the darkest times, the way forward is bright and clear.

In the corporate world, such leaders are invaluable. They're not just managers but visionaries, champions of hope, and architects of a future built on belief and ambition. Their optimism becomes the bedrock upon which organizations innovate, teams collaborate, and ideas flourish. It's a culture where setbacks are just setups for comebacks, challenges are greeted with enthusiasm, and every member feels valued and inspired.

As we habitually foster a positive mindset, let others look to us to point them in the same direction. In nurturing a positive mindset, we're not just leading; we're illuminating paths, uplifting spirits, and crafting a legacy that stands as a testament to the transformative power of positive leadership.

Anchoring the Habits of Resilience
and Overcoming Challenges

Leadership is not merely about titles or positions. At its core, it's about resilience, determination, and unwavering commitment. The theme of this chapter, "Resilience and Overcoming Challenges," resonates deeply with the essence of leadership, emphasizing the importance of facing adversity with strength and grace.

Throughout this chapter, we've ventured through various landscapes of leadership. We've understood that resilience is not about avoiding challenges but growing stronger through them. Leaders who genuinely shine are those who view every obstacle as an opportunity to learn and every setback as a lesson.

A positive mindset, as we've seen, is more than just an optimistic outlook—it's a driving force that pushes us to achieve greatness. Such positivity ripples outward, igniting perseverance and innovation and shaping a belief in the transformative power of challenges.

Handling stress and pressure with poise has shown us true leaders maintain balance even during storms. They guide their teams calmly, offering them strength and assurance and helping them find solutions even in the most challenging times.

We've also delved into the richness of learning from our missteps. Every mistake offers wisdom, and every failure is a step closer to success. Leaders who recognize this grow personally and inspire those around them to see potential in every challenge.

The essence of leadership isn't just about personal achievements. It's about impacting others positively, creating a legacy of change, and guiding with a purpose. As we've explored, leaders driven by purpose focus on the larger picture, aligning their actions with values that benefit the community.

And as we've discussed the importance of a positive mindset, we've seen how such optimism becomes a guiding light, steering us through uncertainties and motivating us to pursue excellence regardless of the odds.

Understanding failure, as we've learned, is not about accepting defeat but about recognizing its role in shaping our success. Embracing these moments of challenge refines us, teaching us invaluable lessons about resilience and growth.

As we conclude this chapter, let's carry forward its core message—that leadership is a journey of continuous learning, adaptation, and dedication. Let's strive to face every challenge with grace, let every difficulty mold us, and emerge from adversity stronger and more inspired.

As we transition to the next topic, let's remember the resilience and strength that have brought us here and use them as our compass for the path ahead, always striving for the pinnacle of leadership excellence.

CHAPTER 9

Ethics and Integrity

INTRODUCTION
The Moral Compass of Leadership

Ethics and integrity shine as pivotal touchstones of leadership, where every choice can echo into eternity, and every action leaves a footprint. Like a compass faithfully pointing north, these twin pillars guide leaders through rugged terrain, ensuring decisions honor a code higher than mere convenience or gain.

Leadership isn't just about reaching milestones. It's about the journey, the lives touched along the way, and the legacy etched into the sands of time. This chapter invites you to take a deep dive into the very soul of leadership—the ethical foundations that distinguish the great from the merely good. We'll uncover the commitment to values that rise above personal interests, respect every individual's worth, and birth environments of trust and authenticity.

Ethics and integrity aren't lofty theories or optional extras. They are the lifeblood of leadership, resonating across borders and cultures. Every leader wields a potent blend of power and influence. With it comes a solemn responsibility—to guide with wisdom, compassion, and an unwavering dedication to the broader good. With a clear moral compass, leaders can traverse the intricate web of choices, championing transparency and justice.

This chapter unveils the myriad facets of ethics and integrity, illustrating their profound impact on leaders, teams, and society. You'll gain insights into the core tenets of ethical behavior, witness the transformative power of exemplary leadership, and grasp the bond that ties integrity to trust. Stories of visionary leaders will punctuate our journey, offering inspiration and tangible lessons.

True leadership isn't a solo act; it's a symphony of collective responsibility. It's about safeguarding timeless principles, much as a lighthouse stands resolute, guiding ships through turbulent waters. Ethical leadership isn't just about doing well—it's about doing right, ensuring our actions mirror our values and our contributions resonate beyond our immediate circle.

Let this chapter be more than a mere read. Let it be a reflection and a reaffirmation of the very essence of leadership that molds character and charts the course of legacies. As we navigate the depths of leadership's ethical core, may we be continually inspired to champion the highest standards and carve pathways of enduring integrity.

LEAD WITH HONESTY

"Honesty is the first chapter in the book of wisdom."

—Thomas Jefferson

eadership is a complex combination of influence, outcomes, and trust. Honesty is the fundamental basis of everything. Thomas Jefferson's words continue to resonate with us, emphasizing the importance of leadership that values truth over pretense. This serves as a powerful reminder of the inherent strength that comes from being honest. This power not only builds strong trust but also creates genuine connections and guides leaders towards ethical excellence. Leading with honesty means consistently embracing the truth, championing transparency, and maintaining unwavering ethical standards.

Authentic leadership is not about naivety; it's about genuine representation. It's about letting go of masks and embracing vulnerability, revealing one's true self. Leaders who operate from a place of authenticity create an atmosphere where trust isn't a bonus; it's a given. They walk the talk, ensuring their actions are a clear reflection of their values.

At the heart of leadership lies the power to guide, inspire, and influence. When rooted in honesty, this power multiplies. Such leaders don't just direct; they cultivate trust, promote open dialogue, and put ethics at the forefront of decisions.

Leading with honesty is like the North Star in a vast night sky. While other stars may waver or fade, the North Star remains constant and true, providing unwavering guidance to travelers lost in the darkness. Just as navigators rely on this beacon to find their way, teams look to honest leaders for direction, clarity, and integrity amidst the uncertainties of their journey.

In the dynamic world of business, honest leadership creates a sturdy foundation. It builds trust, encourages open communication, and fosters a culture of shared goals and values. When honesty becomes an organization's cornerstone, it evolves from being just a trait to a driving force.

In our efforts to be impactful and honest leaders, let's remember that true leadership is not defined by titles but by character. By embracing honesty, we're crafting more than just successful outcomes; we're molding legacies rooted in trust, integrity, and meaningful connections.

HABIT

UPHOLD MORAL PRINCIPLES

"Don't be seduced into thinking that that which does not make a profit is without value."

—Arthur Miller

At the heart of leadership lies the delicate balance between decisions and values. Amidst the ever-evolving landscape of leadership, upholding moral principles stands firm as a guiding star, ensuring ethical actions remain central to all decisions. Arthur Miller's poignant words remind us that true leadership goes beyond immediate returns, championing the enduring essence of moral conviction. This conviction molds character, anchors purpose, and steers leaders toward a legacy of long-lasting significance.

Upholding morals isn't about strict adherence; it's about strength of character. While a leader's primary role may involve driving results, it's equally essential to influence and leave a positive mark on society's ethical ideology. Like a seasoned sailor maneuvering through a storm, leaders grounded in moral principles sail with certainty, their decisions deeply rooted in ethical foundations.

Central to this habit is recognizing leadership as both a privilege and a responsibility. Embracing moral principles signifies understanding that leadership's true impact goes beyond immediate achievements. It's found in the legacy left behind, one that's built on ethical decisions and meaningful actions. Such leaders foster a culture where every decision is backed by moral commitment, actions mirror values, and endeavors are a testament to integrity.

Leadership grounded in morals is a journey of both conviction and inspiration. It's about navigating challenges with an unwavering ethical compass and igniting that fire in others. Such leaders become standard-bearers of values-driven leadership, motivating teams to realize that ethics isn't an added benefit but a vital cornerstone.

Imagine a gardener meticulously caring for every plant, ensuring each grows strong and blossoms. Similarly, leaders upholding moral principles care for the ethical landscape of their domain, ensuring values are not just discussed but deeply ingrained. Their actions reflect a deep commitment, emphasizing that success isn't just about hitting milestones but is deeply intertwined with ethical foundations.

In business, these leaders are not just strategists but also guardians. They instill a culture where decisions are evaluated by their profit margins and ethical merits. Their influence promotes an environment where values are more than words; they're the essence of every action.

As we champion the cause of upholding moral principles, let's light the path with our unwavering commitment to ethics. Inspired by past legacies, let's remember that the heart of leadership lies not in fleeting achievements but in the transformational power of ethical principles. By staying true to these morals, we not only elevate our journey but also craft an enduring legacy of ethical leadership, positive change, and profound impact.

HABIT

ACT WITH INTEGRITY

> *"Integrity is choosing courage over comfort; choosing what is right over what is fun, fast, or easy; and choosing to practice our values rather than simply professing them."*
>
> —Brené Brown

A cting with integrity is not a quest for flawlessness but a commitment to authenticity. It's acknowledging that, as leaders, we may not always have all the answers, but a set of unwavering core values always drives us. Like a compass that remains resolute in pointing north, a leader with integrity remains grounded, ensuring actions align with principles even when the environment shifts.

Understanding that true leadership is about influence rooted in trust and respect is central to this habit. Such trust isn't bestowed by titles or positions but is earned over time through consistent and authentic actions. Leaders who embrace integrity know that trust, once broken, is hard to mend. Therefore, they maintain a culture where promises are kept, and core values are spoken and lived daily.

Acting with integrity is about more than making the right choices; it's about standing by them, especially when they're difficult or unpopular.

These leaders are beacons of trust, inspiring others to understand that genuine leadership isn't about rhetoric; it's about the congruence between words and deeds. Their actions lay the foundation for an environment that values authenticity, where individuals are inspired to act in alignment with shared values, driving a collective vision forward.

Acting with integrity is like the keystone in an arch. Though it may seem just one piece among many, it holds the entire structure together, and without it, everything would crumble. Just as the arch leans on the keystone for support, so does the foundation of trust rely on our consistent actions of integrity.

In the business world, leaders grounded in integrity don't just drive results; they sculpt cultures. They instill an ethos where ethical decisions are the norm, transparency prevails, and the organization's moral compass aligns with its strategic direction. Their influence permeates every layer, fostering an environment where integrity is the bedrock, not an afterthought.

As we champion the cause of acting with integrity, let's remain rooted in authenticity. Inspired by leaders who've shaped history with their unwavering values, let's remember that genuine leadership isn't about fleeting accolades but about the lasting legacy of trust and respect. By committing to integrity, we don't just lead organizations and teams; we shape cultures, influence perspectives, and leave an enduring footprint of authentic leadership.

HABIT

BE ACCOUNTABLE FOR ACTIONS

"The time is always right to do what is right."

—Martin Luther King Jr.

I n the complex world of leadership, taking responsibility for your actions is a sign of real leadership. Martin Luther King Jr.'s wise words remind us that being a leader with integrity isn't just about making the right decisions; it's also about taking responsibility for them, no matter how they turn out. Leadership is more than just making decisions; it's also about taking on the responsibilities that come with those decisions and living by the core values that guide every action.

Central to this habit is recognizing that leadership is less about decision-making and more about owning and understanding its implications. Leaders who value accountability understand that trust isn't just about making the right decisions; it's about holding oneself accountable for them. Accountability is not about attributing fault but about embracing responsibility. This commitment to answerability paves the way for a culture where every action has a face and a name behind it, fostering a sense of authenticity and ethical commitment.

Accountability is a celebration of empowerment. Leaders who embody this value inspire teams to understand that leadership is less about perfection and more about learning from imperfections. Such leaders don't run from challenges; they own them, offering a paradigm where accountability is synonymous with growth and progress.

Imagine a bridge—anchored firmly, supporting countless journeys, weathering storms, yet unwavering in its purpose. Such is a leader who stands accountable—offering guidance, support, and above all, a sense of reliability. Just as bridges connect, leaders with accountability bridge gaps between actions and outcomes, choices and consequences, creating an environment where responsibility isn't shirked but embraced.

In the corporate world, leaders grounded in accountability don't merely drive objectives; they shape cultures. They instill an ethos where every decision is owned, where responsibility is a badge worn with pride, and where the collective conscience of the organization aligns with ethical and moral imperatives. Their influence creates a symphony of actions and responsibilities, where accountability becomes the rhythm that synchronizes an organization's heartbeat.

As we champion the essence of being accountable for our actions, let's wear responsibility as our armor and remember that true leadership isn't about steering clear of errors but about navigating through them with grace and accountability. Embracing this habit fortifies our journey and imprints a legacy—one that's defined by responsibility, trust, and lasting influence.

HABIT

BUILD A CULTURE OF TRANSPARENCY

"Transparency, honesty, kindness, good stewardship,
even humor, work in businesses at all times."

—John Gerzema

Leadership is based on relationships and trust, and the culture of transparency emphasizes the importance of honesty, openness, and respect. As John Gerzema said, it reminds us that true leadership is open and honest. We learn about building a culture of transparency and are asked to plan a path of real communication, heartfelt connections, and ethical conversation.

Creating a culture of transparency isn't about sharing all but about cultivating an ambiance of trust where pertinent information is disseminated purposefully and where candidness thrives. Like the dawn dispelling shadows, transparent leaders eradicate ambiguities, lighting the path of clear communication, nurturing an atmosphere of trust, and bonding teams with the adhesive of mutual respect and understanding.

Central to this habit is the realization that leadership thrives on connectivity. Authenticity, rather than concealment, is the bedrock of enduring relationships. Leaders dedicated to transparency appreciate the essence of open dialogue, crafting an environment where every voice matters, every query receives an answer, and every individual feels seen and heard.

The pursuit of transparency is, indeed, an odyssey of empowerment. Leaders championing this cause become the standard-bearers of genuine communication, steering their organizations towards a culture where information isn't just hoarded but shared, fostering collaboration, enhancing trust, and bolstering collective momentum.

Leading a transparent culture is like tending a lush botanical garden under a glass dome. Each plant, representing a team member or idea, thrives under the clear canopy in the unfiltered sunlight. The transparent glass dome lets the outside world see the beauty and growth inside and gives every plant an equal chance to thrive. The leader tends to each plant, addresses concerns, and fosters trust and unity like a gardener.

Champions of transparency don't just lead; they inspire. Through their dedication to openness, they sculpt workplaces where candid communication is celebrated, barriers to information crumble, and collective wisdom shapes the organization's ethos. Their impact echoes throughout the organization, molding a culture where transparency isn't an afterthought but the ethos defining collective action and thought.

As we pledge to foster a culture of transparency, may we light the lanterns of honest discourse and mutual respect. Drawing wisdom from luminaries like Gerzema, let's remember that the essence of leadership is not in its title but in its ability to foster genuine connections. In championing transparency, we don't just shape organizational cultures; we curate legacies rooted in trust, authenticity and an unyielding spirit of unity.

Anchoring the Habits of Ethics and Integrity

Leadership is about making impactful decisions and developing a character that will determine where we go. This chapter, "Ethics and Integrity," has gone into great detail about the moral foundations of leadership. We've successfully navigated the complex terrain at the crossroads of merit, genuineness, and lasting influence by keeping ethics and integrity as our north star. Leaders rely on these qualities in the same way that explorers do when venturing into uncharted territory.

This chapter took us on a deep journey into what it truly means to lead with morality. We've looked at the essence of leading transparently, acting with integrity, and championing honesty. These aren't just lofty concepts; they are the very tools that mold character, foster trust, and help create a legacy far beyond any individual accolade.

Being a leader means recognizing that ethical behavior isn't an optional add-on—it's a fundamental responsibility. It's not just about achieving goals; it's about how we go about them, the values we uphold, and standing firm even when the going gets tough.

Ethics and integrity aren't just limited to this chapter; they're part of the very DNA of genuine leadership. They aren't passing phases but timeless foundations upon which lasting leadership stands. These principles enable us to act with courage, respect everyone's worth, and stay true to ourselves and our teams.

As we step out of this chapter, let's keep the essence of ethics and integrity alive, letting them light our way. Let's be inspired by those leaders who've walked before us, creating paths of honor, trust, and positive change. By living these values, we're not just being better leaders; we're building legacies that matter.

Moving forward, let's remember the core messages here. Leadership is as much about the journey as the destination, and it's shaped by our values, authenticity, and ethics. With this guiding moral compass, we're set to embrace what lies ahead, tackling new challenges and continuing our mission: to inspire, to guide, and to create a lasting legacy of integrity.

CHAPTER 10

Legacy and Impact

INTRODUCTION
Forging a Lasting Imprint

A s we weave our way through the intricate narratives of leadership, where every action has weight and influence, we arrive at lasting legacies and meaningful impacts. This isn't just another chapter; it's an investigation into the timeless echoes of our leadership choices. We're about to go deeper, beyond mere accomplishments, to learn how true, purposeful leadership creates ripples that outlast us.

Legacy and impact aren't just jargon. They encapsulate the very soul of a leader's journey. Think of a painter carefully choosing each color and each stroke, crafting a masterpiece. Similarly, leaders weave their choices, experiences, and values into tapestries that inspire and influence long after they're gone. Here, in "Legacy and Impact," we'll chart the course of such leadership, inspired by luminaries of the past and conscious of the future we're molding with our actions today.

This chapter isn't just about leadership's purpose but also its lasting effect. We'll delve into what it means to lead with purpose and how transformative it can be when our actions are aligned with a larger vision. Whether it's defining an organization's ethos or sparking societal change, the legacy of leadership is far-reaching.

It's not always about groundbreaking actions; often, it's the daily interactions, the upheld values, and the built relationships. Like a small stone sending ripples across a pond, every decision a leader makes has its own ripple effect, touching hearts, minds, and the broader world. Throughout this chapter, we'll unearth these subtle yet profound ways leaders leave their mark.

Our leadership journey is both a privilege and a responsibility. As we delve into this chapter, we're prompted to ponder the lasting trails we're carving. It's not about titles or accolades; it's about the souls we influence, the values we breathe life into, and the environments we nurture.

Chapter 10, in essence, is a reflection and a challenge: How will we be remembered? What mark do we wish to make? By studying the legacies of impactful leaders, we're encouraged to align our path with purpose, embrace the weight of our influence, and aim for long-standing, positive change.

As we uncover what it means to leave a legacy, let's journey with intention, seeking wisdom from the past and keeping an eye on the legacy we wish to craft. This is more than leadership for today—it's about shaping tomorrow. By internalizing this chapter's ethos, we aim for not just success but significance, creating echoes of purposeful leadership that will resonate for generations.

HABIT

GIVE BACK TO THE COMMUNITY

"We make a living by what we get, but we make a life by what we give."

—Winston Churchill

eadership is not merely a position or title but a responsibility. It's about the difference we make, the lives we touch, and the legacy we leave behind. In leadership, giving back to the community stands out as a symbol of true compassion and an unwavering commitment to uplifting others.

Giving back to the community is an endorsement of empathy, not just charity—a recognition that leadership is about more than just personal gain, but also about the collective well-being of those we serve. Leaders who prioritize giving back, like a river, become conduits of positive change, channeling their influence to enrich the lives of others and create a ripple effect of compassion. They become architects of unity under their guidance, embodying the unwavering spirit that not only thrives on success but also transforms that success into a force that uplifts, inspires, and fosters collective growth.

Central to this principle is the notion that leadership is service. It's not about the accolades, the titles, or tangible rewards. It's about the lives we better, the hands we extend in assistance, and the positive ripples we create. No matter how small, every act can be a catalyst for change, a gesture of compassion, and an opportunity to make a difference.

Consider the metaphor of a tree, which stretches its branches to provide shelter, shade, and nourishment to those in its vicinity. Leaders who give back to their communities grow into metaphorical trees, inspiring teams to thrive, cultivating a sense of belonging, and creating an environment in which everyone's well-being is a collective responsibility. Their actions, like trees, provide the nurturing touch of ethical leadership and the wisdom to recognize that leadership is about contributing to the growth of the community, not just personal gain.

In the business world, leaders prioritizing community involvement pave the way for lasting impact. They foster cultures where helping isn't an afterthought but a fundamental value. Such environments encourage collaboration, drive positive change, and emphasize the collective over the individual.

So, as we delve into the habit of community involvement, let's remember that leadership isn't just about reaching the top. It's about lifting others as we climb. By giving back, we aren't just creating a momentary difference; we're building a lasting legacy of kindness, unity, and transformative leadership.

HABIT

LEAD WITH EMPATHY

"The greatest leaders are those who lead with love and empathy."

—Robin S. Sharma

At its core, leadership is about understanding and connection. Empathy—the ability to truly feel and understand the emotions of others—is the golden thread that binds leaders to their teams. Robin S. Sharma's quote captures the essence of this sentiment, emphasizing that leadership transcends authority and taps into human connection.

True empathy is more than just sympathy or mere understanding. It's about genuinely feeling for others, standing in their shoes, and seeing the world through their eyes. This isn't a sign of vulnerability or weakness but of immense strength and authenticity.

Imagine a conductor seamlessly merging the notes from various instruments to create a harmonious tune. Similarly, an empathetic leader orchestrates a team's diverse emotions, aspirations, and perspectives into a cohesive, powerful force. Such leaders provide direction and ensure each team member feels understood and valued.

This habit is all about recognizing that genuine leadership is rooted in connection. Leaders who prioritize empathy don't merely give directives;

they listen, relate, and build bridges of trust and understanding. They create an environment where every interaction is a chance to genuinely connect, every decision is made with deep consideration, and every action speaks volumes about their commitment to their team's well-being.

Think of a quilt, with each patch representing a unique experience yet all woven together to provide warmth and comfort. Leaders who practice empathy are like quilt-makers, stitching together their team members' diverse experiences and perspectives to form a cohesive and supportive unit. Their leadership is characterized by inclusivity, validation, and a genuine concern for the well-being of others.

In the corporate world, such leaders have an enduring impact. They foster a culture of understanding and kindness and ensure emotional well-being is given as much priority as business goals. In these organizations, empathy is not just an encouraged trait; it's a way of life, shaping interactions, decisions, and legacies.

As we delve deeper into the importance of leading with empathy, let's remember that leadership's true essence isn't just about influence or authority. It's about understanding, caring for, and uplifting those we lead. By adopting this approach, leaders don't just achieve targets; they touch lives, creating a legacy of compassion, unity, and profound impact.

HABIT

INSPIRE OTHERS TO LEAD

"The greatest leader is not necessarily the one who does the greatest things. He is the one that gets the people to do the greatest things."

—Ronald Reagan

The ability to inspire others to take the helm emerges as the pinnacle of empowerment. Ronald Reagan's insight captures this beautifully, emphasizing that leadership transcends personal accomplishments. The true essence of a leader lies in their ability to nurture, guide, and inspire others to achieve greatness. When we learn how to best inspire others to lead, we understand that leadership isn't about being at the forefront but about lighting the path for others to follow.

True leadership is not about holding onto power or being constantly in the spotlight. It's about recognizing potential in others and providing them with the tools, knowledge, and encouragement to step up and lead. Just as a gardener carefully tills the soil and nurtures seeds to blossom, leaders must cultivate an environment where potential leaders can grow and thrive.

At its heart, this habit is about empowerment. A leader's true strength lies not in how many followers they have but in how many leaders they help create. By championing this cause, they foster a culture where leadership is shared, achievements are celebrated together, and every individual is given a chance to shine.

Think of leadership as a relay race where the baton is passed from one person to another. Each individual runs their leg of the race but also ensures the next person is prepared and well-positioned to continue. Leaders who inspire others are like the best relay racers, ensuring smooth transitions and rooting for their team's success even when they're not running.

Leaders who champion this habit of inspiring others to lead create a ripple effect in business. They build organizations where mentorship is treasured, leadership qualities are nurtured, and every individual is viewed as a potential leader. Such organizations don't just succeed in the short term; they build legacies.

As we embark on this journey of inspiring others to lead, let's remember that the most significant legacies are not built on personal achievements but on the leaders we help create. By inspiring others, we're not just building a team or an organization; we're shaping the future of leadership, ensuring that the torch of inspiration, guidance, and empowerment continues to be passed on. Through this habit, we cement our legacy of being great leaders and leaving behind a lineage of empowered and inspiring leaders.

HABIT

CONTINUOUSLY EVOLVE

> *"The biggest risk is not evolving."*
>
> —Reed Hastings

The act of constant evolution is crucial in the ever-shifting symphony of leadership, where development is the crescendo and adaptation is the persistent beat. Reed Hastings's insight is a timely reminder that leadership is not about clinging to the past but looking forward to the future.

Genuine leadership does not rest on its success. It is about accepting that the only constant is change and that embracing change is critical to remaining relevant and ahead of the competition. Leaders must remain fluid, adjusting their strategies and mindsets to the challenges and opportunities that come their way, much like a river that flows, bending and adapting to its surroundings.

At the core of this habit is the acknowledgment that the world doesn't wait. New challenges arise, technologies disrupt, and societal values shift. Leaders who make continuous evolution a cornerstone of their leadership philosophy understand that they must be lifelong learners, curious, and ready to adapt. Continuously evolving doesn't mean changing for the sake of changing. It means being acutely aware of the environment, being proactive rather than reactive, and ensuring that growth and innovation are ingrained in the very fabric of an organization. Leaders who embody this habit are not just navigators but explorers, charting new territories and pioneering change.

In business, continuously evolving leaders are the ones who go the furthest. They're at the forefront of innovation, driving their organizations towards new horizons, and always looking for the next challenge or opportunity. They foster environments where change is not feared but embraced, innovation is a daily practice, and every team member is empowered to contribute to the collective evolution.

Embracing the habit of continuously evolving is more than just a strategy; it's a mindset. It's about understanding that the journey of leadership is never static. It's about inspiring those around us with the passion for exploration, the hunger for learning, and the resilience to adapt. In doing so, we craft legacies that resonate not just for their achievements but for their forward momentum, the paths they've paved, and the doors they've opened for the next generation to explore.

In a world that's evolving faster than ever, let us remain the torchbearers of change, innovation champions, and continuous growth advocates. Because in the end, the real legacy of leadership isn't just about where we've been but where we're headed and the paths we carve for others to follow.

HABIT

LEAVE A LASTING LEGACY

"Your work is going to fill a large part of your life, and the only way to be truly satisfied is to do what you believe is great work."

—Steve Jobs

A leader's actions are like the strokes of a painter's brush; together, they create something beautiful. Where these brushstrokes are thoughtful, significant, and imbued with intent, a portrait of an enduring legacy is created. Leadership paths etched with intention, passion, and a desire to leave a mark that lasts are the most fulfilling, as demonstrated by Steve Jobs's insight.

A lasting legacy is not a tribute to oneself. Instead, it's a testament to impact. It goes beyond mere personal achievements and delves into the profound, creating a ripple effect that touches lives, influences thought and shapes the trajectory of futures yet unwritten.

Central to this habit is the knowledge that true leadership is not about fleeting accolades but about anchoring one's actions in purpose and passion. Such leaders understand that they are part of a bigger picture, where their contributions today light the torch for the leaders of tomorrow. This legacy is born from consistent efforts, a commitment to values, and an insatiable drive to make a difference. It's about laying the foundations for future generations to build, innovate, and thrive.

Legacy-building leaders serve as pillars of strength, instilling hope, fostering growth, and leading with an ethical compass that shines brightly, much like the guiding light of a lighthouse. They serve as beacons, illuminating the path and inspiring those in their wake to aim higher, dream bigger, and strive harder. Their leadership narrative transcends personal accolades and creates an environment where every team member feels empowered, valued, and part of a purpose larger than themselves.

Leaders who aim for lasting legacies don't just scale organizational heights; they mold cultures of integrity, innovation, and purpose-driven ambition. Their decisions are not solely based on short-term gains but on long-term impacts, ensuring that their leadership tale is one of transformation, ethical stewardship, and boundless inspiration.

As we step habitually understand legacy leadership, let it be with the solemn knowledge that the legacies we leave are not just about our stories but about the stories of those we've touched, influenced, and inspired. It's about creating an impact so rich in purpose that it serves as a guiding star for generations to come. In this endeavor, let us find fulfillment not in personal milestones but in the timeless imprints we leave behind, crafting a narrative of purpose, passion, and profound legacy.

Anchoring the Habits of Legacy and Impact

Every leader begins their journey with a blank canvas. Over time, with experience, wisdom, and intention, they begin to paint their legacy, stroke by stroke, decision by decision. As we close the chapter on legacy and impact, we are left with a vibrant mosaic of leadership habits, each one revealing a facet of the leader's soul and the impact they wish to leave behind.

The chapter's narrative encapsulates the essence of leadership beyond titles, achievements, or accolades. It celebrates leadership striving for a higher purpose, which reverberates through time, leaving an echo of inspiration, transformation, and positive change for generations to come.

The idea of giving back underscores that leadership is not a solitary journey. It's a collaborative dance where leaders extend their hand to uplift others, understanding that collective prosperity and well-being enrich the fabric of our communities and societies. Through empathy, leaders bridge gaps, erase boundaries, and create spaces where every voice is heard, valued, and respected.

As leaders, our task isn't just to lead and inspire leadership in others. This chapter has emphasized the role of a leader as a torchbearer—one who lights the path for others, showing them the way while encouraging them to find their unique journey of impact. Continual personal and organizational evolution emerges as a non-negotiable trait, emphasizing the idea that stagnation is the antithesis of growth, innovation, and progress.

Legacy is the culmination of one's life's work, but its essence lies in the seeds one plants for the future. True leaders don't just aim for immediate results; they strive to build foundations that will support, nurture, and inspire long after they have moved on.

As this chapter comes to a close, it serves as a reminder—a beacon— urging us to pause, reflect, and realign. It encourages us to look beyond the immediate horizon, dream bigger, act with purpose, and lead with an unwavering commitment to leaving the world a better place.

The trust we have built on our leadership journey is a testament to our values, decisions, and impact. It's a constant reminder that leadership is both an honor and a responsibility. And as we venture forward, may we always be guided by empathy, innovation, resilience, and legacy, creating a world where leadership is not just about the here and now but about shaping a brighter, more impactful future for all.

EPILOGUE

As we close the final chapter of "50 Habits of Highly Successful Business Leaders" we find ourselves at the crossroads of reflection and anticipation. This journey of wisdom, inspiration, and growth has led us through the intricate web of leadership, revealing the habits that define exceptional leaders and their enduring impact on the world.

The threads of self-mastery, communication, collaboration, and decision-making have been woven into a fabric of excellence, guiding us toward a deeper understanding of what it takes to lead with purpose and integrity. We have explored leadership and team building, strategic thinking, execution, and influence, discovering the transformative power of each habit to shape organizations, drive innovation, and inspire greatness.

Resilience, ethics, and legacy have illuminated our path, reminding us that true leadership extends beyond success to embrace the legacy we leave behind—a legacy of impact, empowerment, and positive change. In these pages, we have been reminded that leadership is not a solitary journey; it is a collective endeavor that transcends time, guided by the insights of those who have blazed a trail before us.

As we stand at the closing of this chapter, let us carry forward the lessons learned, the wisdom gleaned, and the principles embraced. Let us be the leaders who elevate our communities, organizations, and industries by embodying the habits that define excellence. Let us inspire, empower, and shape a world where ethical leadership, innovation, and purposeful action become the cornerstones of success.

Our journey does not end here; it is an invitation to continue exploring, growing, and striving for leadership greatness. With each new day, we have the opportunity to elevate ourselves, our teams, and our organizations to new heights of achievement and positive impact.

As we move forward, let us embrace our roles as stewards of leadership, committed to fostering a culture of growth, collaboration, and positive change.

And so, as we turn the final page, let us embark on our individual journeys, armed with the habits, insights, and inspiration to become leaders who leave a lasting legacy—a legacy of impact, purpose, and unwavering commitment to making the world a better place.

50 QUOTES

"The only thing that's keeping you from getting what you
want is the story you keep telling yourself."

–Tony Robbins

"The biggest room in the world is the room for improvement."

–Helmut Schmidt

"An unexamined life is not worth living."

–Socrates

"Success is not final, failure is not fatal: It is the
courage to continue that counts."

–Winston Churchill

"You may delay, but time will not."

–Benjamin Franklin

"The most important thing in communication is hearing what isn't said."

–Peter Drucker

"The only way to do great work is to love what you do."

–Steve Jobs

"Your culture is your brand."

–Tony Hsieh

"Great leaders are willing to sacrifice their own interests for the good of the group."

–John C. Maxwell

"People don't care how much you know until they know how much you care."

–Theodore Roosevelt

"The price of greatness is responsibility."

–Winston Churchill

"In God we trust; all others must bring data."

–W. Edwards Deming

"Strength lies in differences, not in similarities."

–Stephen R. Covey

"The biggest risk is not taking any risk."

–Mark Zuckerberg

"It's not the strongest of the species that survive, nor the most intelligent, but the one most responsive to change."

–Charles Darwin

"You don't lead by pointing and telling people some place to go. You lead by going to that place and making a case."

–Ken Kesey

"Leadership is not about being in charge. It's about taking care of those in your charge."

–Simon Sinek

"Trust is the glue of life. It's the most essential ingredient in effective communication. It's the foundational principle that holds all relationships."

–Stephen R. Covey

"Innovation distinguishes between a leader and a follower."

–Steve Jobs

"The best executive is the one who has sense enough to pick good men to do what he wants done, and self-restraint enough to keep from meddling with them while they do it."

–Theodore Roosevelt

"You have to set goals that are almost out of reach. If you set a goal that is attainable without much work or thought, you are stuck with something below your true talent and potential."

–Steve Garvey

"The difference between a successful person and others is not a lack of strength, not a lack of knowledge, but rather a lack in will."

–Vince Lombardi

"The capacity to learn is a gift; the ability to learn is a skill; the willingness to learn is a choice."

–Brian Herbert

"Your network is your net worth."

–Porter Gale

"In the short term, you can fool yourself and others. In the long run, the market will tell you whether you are delivering value or not."

–Jeff Bezos

"The path to success is to take massive, determined action."

–Tony Robbins

"Efficiency is doing things right. Effectiveness is doing the right things."

–Peter Drucker

"Don't count the days, make the days count."

–Muhammad Ali

"You can do anything, but not everything."

–David Allen

"The best way to predict the future is to create it."

–Peter Drucker

"If you just communicate, you can get by. But if you communicate skillfully, you can work miracles."

–Jim Rohn

"You can't do today's job with yesterday's methods and be in business tomorrow."

–George W. Bush

"You can't make decisions based on fear and the possibility of what might happen."

–Michelle Obama

"I've learned that people will forget what you said, people will forget what you did, but people will never forget how you made them feel."

–Maya Angelou

"Influence is the key to any leadership."

–John C. Maxwell

"Success is stumbling from failure to failure with no loss of enthusiasm."

–Winston Churchill

"The best way to find yourself is to lose yourself in the service of others."

–Mahatma Gandhi

"The greatest weapon against stress is our ability
to choose one thought over another."

–William James

"The only real mistake is the one from which we learn nothing."

–Henry Ford

"Optimism is the faith that leads to achievement. Nothing
can be done without hope and confidence."

–Helen Keller

"Honesty is the first chapter in the book of wisdom."

–Thomas Jefferson

"Don't be seduced into thinking that that which
does not make a profit is without value."

–Arthur Miller

"Integrity is choosing courage over comfort; choosing what is
right over what is fun, fast, or easy; and choosing to practice
our values rather than simply professing them."

–Brené Brown

"The time is always right to do what is right."

–Martin Luther King Jr.

"Transparency, honesty, kindness, good stewardship,
even humor, work in businesses at all times."

–John Gerzema

"We make a living by what we get, but we make a life by what we give."

–Winston Churchill

"The greatest leaders are those who lead with love and empathy."

–Robin S. Sharma

"The greatest leader is not necessarily the one who does the greatest things. He is the one that gets the people to do the greatest things."

–Ronald Reagan

"The biggest risk is not evolving."

–Reed Hastings

"Your work is going to fill a large part of your life, and the only way to be truly satisfied is to do what you believe is great work."

–Steve Jobs

END NOTE

A s I wrote the insights in "50 Habits of Highly Successful Business Leaders," I imagined each of you, from budding managers to seasoned CEOs, eagerly looking for that next step or affirmation on your leadership journey. Every habit and inspiration message in this book is meant to inspire, motivate, and harness what it means to be a true leader.

This book was my window into understanding what makes leaders successful and truly inspiring. I hope, in turn, it's become a mirror for you, reflecting the vast potential and the spark of purpose that lies within.

Life has taught me that leadership isn't about grand gestures but about everyday actions. The habits we've delved into are not just to be read but to be lived, challenging you daily to be better, to influence positively, and to craft a brighter tomorrow. And while the road to great leadership is lined with both challenges and triumphs, remember that each step adds to your unique story.

Whether you're just setting out or looking to scale new peaks in your leadership journey, I hope this book is your trusted guide and your comforting companion. Because in the end, it's not just about business success; it's about the legacy of change and inspiration we leave behind.

Thank you for allowing me to be a part of your journey in building meaningful habits. May your leadership journey touch hearts, drive change, and make a difference, not just in boardrooms but in the very fabric of our society.

With heartfelt appreciation and a shared
vision of a better tomorrow,
Matthew Lin

ABOUT THE AUTHOR:

Matthew is a design architect and property developer by day and an ardent self-help writer by night. With a robust background in architecture and property development, Matthew brings a unique perspective to his work: combining creativity, business acumen, and a desire to inspire and empower others through his writing. He is also a dedicated proptech enthusiast and enjoys constantly exploring innovative technologies to enhance the real estate industry.

Matthew's varied life experiences have helped shape his fascinating and motivational persona. After studying architecture in Auckland, New Zealand, he spent more than 10 years working as a design architect in Singapore before shifting gears as a property developer in Thailand for the last 15 years. He is currently working to develop an online platform designed to simplify the real estate ecosystem.

Matthew's expertise extends beyond the realms of blueprints, building sites, and technology. Not only has he consulted numerous businesses—offering 1-on-1 coaching services and advice on general business, real estate, and technology—but he has also supported countless experts and amateurs alike as they seek to better understand their respective industries.

Matthew's path is proof of the positive impact that optimism, creativity, and self-assurance can have on one's life. His life's tale is a motivating example of how anyone can achieve his/her goals with the appropriate attitude and the drive to keep plugging away at them. Matthew's story has inspired people of various backgrounds to believe in themselves and their abilities and take risks in pursuit of their goals.

Current Book List:

- 50 Habits of Highly Successful Business Leaders   (2023)
  The Roadmap to Success and Fulfillment

- Mastering the Art Of Business Networking   (2023)
  The 8 Essential Steps to Creating Lasting Connections.

- Master Procrastination & Achieve Your Goals   (2023)
  8 Essential Steps to Regain Control of Your Life

Matthew resides in Chiang Mai, Thailand with his wife and two children. You can reach out to him at www.linkedin.com/in/matthew-lin-72061b282. He would love to hear from you!

www.ingramcontent.com/pod-product-compliance
Lightning Source LLC
Chambersburg PA
CBHW072204290526
45794CB00004B/1651